GET WHAT YOU WANT!

"Patricia Fripp is an extraordinary woman. She is a real role model and inspiration to us all. This is a great book, loaded with fast, effective, practical ideas you can use immediately to get better results."
—Brian Tracy, author of *Maximum Achievement*

"Many Fortune 500 companies have benefited from Patricia's advice and enjoyable teaching style. Truly one of the top speakers in North America."
—Ken Blanchard, co-author of *The One Minute Manager*

"In business and in life, Patricia Fripp has the unique ability to take your most timid dreams and turn them into bold and enduring reality. Best of all, she'll give you the courage and conviction to do it!"
—David Garfinkel, co-author of *Guerrilla Marketing for the Imaging Industry*

"Patricia Fripp is one of my role models! She provides great insight into business development and career success. Fripp has energized me to get what I want in my dual career as a best selling author and speaker."
—Susan RoAne, author of *How To Work A Room and What Do I Say Next?*

"Patricia has consistently been a favorite with Aloette Beauty Consultants and Franchisees. Her thoughts in speeches and books are inspiring, practical and entertainingly presented. I'd recommend *Get What You Want!* to everybody."
—Tricia Defibaugh, Chairman of the Board, Aloette Cosmetics

"Patricia Fripp is history in the making. Among the great minds of men…Napoleon Hill, Dale Carnegie, Norman Vincent Peale, Zig Ziglar… Fripp is the reigning Queen of Philosophers. The most charismatic speaker I've ever seen! Enrich your life as I have! Seek your greatest potential! READ THIS BOOK!"
—Dan Maddux, Association Executive, America Payroll Association

"I love this book. I bought 650 copies for my entire group."
—Cathie Calloway, Special Event Coordinator, Kaiser Permanente

"This is my sister. I have watched her career since I was born. Read her book!!!"
—Robert Fripp, King Crimson, DGM Records

GET WHAT YOU WANT!

Patricia Fripp

By the co-author of:

Insights into Excellence
Speaking Secrets of the Masters

Revised edition, copyright ©1998 by Patricia Fripp

PRINTING HISTORY
1988 edition published by H.D.L. Publishing Company
1982 edition published by Harbor Publishing Company

Patricia Fripp
(800) 634-3035
e-mail PFripp@aol.com
http://www.fripp.com

Printed in the United States of America
Library of Congress Catalog Card Number 98-84572
ISBN 0-937539-26-0 (Paperback)
ISBN 0-937539-25-2 (Hardcover)
by
Executive Books
Life Management Services, Inc.
Mechanicsburg, PA

(800) 233-2665

DEDICATION

In memory of my parents Arthur and Edie Fripp who taught me "You can't be too kind or too generous." To my soul mate Robert, my brother. And also to the clients who hire me, my cronies who encourage me, and the audiences who make any inconvenience of traveling worthwhile.

ACKNOWLEDGMENTS

Eleanor Dugan for her invaluable editorial assistance. Patricia Lauterjung and Becky Gordon for their copyediting. Charles Tremendous Jones for his enthusiastic support.

FORWARD

This book is all about possibilities. I hope the words inspire you to look at all the options, choices, opportunities, and potential— the *possibilities*—in your own life.

CONTENTS

CHAPTER 1

If the World Were Perfect

FRIPPICISM

Tell me what you want.
Then show me one week of your life,
and I'll tell you if you'll get it.

Texas multi-millionaire H. L. Hunt was interviewed on a North Carolina television talk show some years back by my friend Ty Boyd. Boyd asked Hunt, "How have you amassed fortunes when most of us are struggling to make a living?"

Hunt, who built the Houston Astrodome, replied, "You have to make up your mind what you want. You have to make up your mind what you are prepared to give up to get it. You have to set your priorities, and then go about your job."

That sounds too simple to be true. But think about it:

Decide what you want.

It amazes me that most people spend more time planning next summer's vacation than they do planning the rest of their lives. What do you want? How do you want your life to be different in the future? What do you want to accomplish in your career, for yourself, or with your family? And what are you willing to do to achieve it?

Define "Success"

Nearly everyone wants to be successful, but few can define it. Does success involve money? On the basis of income, the average twelve-year-old drug dealer is then more successful than Ralph Nader, Mother Teresa, Shakespeare, or Martin Luther King, Jr. Does success mean power over other people's lives? Then a dedicated terrorist is just as successful as Gandhi, Lincoln, or the entire graduating class of a major medical school. Does success mean controlling how people think and act? Then pop stars (as John Lennon noted sadly in his often-misinterpreted remark) are certainly as successful as Jesus.

Obviously few people are eager to be unsuccessful, and just as obviously success needs some rigorous defining. You can start by understanding very specifically what you want.

What do you want? Most people's responses are vague, almost generic. For instance:

"I want more." More what? More than who? Exactly how much? Why? Then what?

"I want things to be better." Better than what? Better how? Better for whom? What are your criteria?

"I want to get ahead." Of whom? How? How will you know when you have gotten there? Then what?

"I want so-and-so to be proud of me." A worthy goal and one that separates humans from amoebas, but are you sure specific actions will produce the desired result? What specifically must you accomplish? How will you feel then? How will you feel when you reach your goal if so-and-so isn't proud of you? Would it make any difference?

"I want people to respect me." The dictionary defines "respect" as "to revere, esteem, or admire." Which specifically do you want? For some people, having respect means people notice, obey, or fear them. Do you want admiration or just attention? Esteem or, in reality, obedience? Do you want to be respected for a specific quality or a specific accomplishment? What are you going to do so people will respond to you in this

positive way? What if you carry out your plan and people don't react the way you want?

My friend, movie reviewer Scott McKain, was interviewing Tom Hanks for station WISH-TV in Indianapolis. He asked Hanks, who won two Academy Awards back to back, "What is success?"

"It's too soon to tell if I will be successful or not," Hanks replied. "To me, success is constantly getting better at your craft and performing at a high level for an extended period of time. Jimmy Stewart, Gregory Peck—those are people who have been successful. Fame is different. Fame does something to your head from which you may never recover. Sure, I get to cut in line at restaurants and airports, but if you think that is success, you are sadly mistaken—as the tragic events of today clearly show." (The interview was taking place in Los Angeles during the infamous O.J. Simpson Bronco chase on the freeway.)

Barbara Walters once asked Oscar-winner Joanne Woodward, "What is success to you?" ("That's easy," I thought, "Being rich, famous, and sleeping with Paul Newman!") But Joanne had a different answer. "Success to me," she said, "would be raising four children who don't need a psychiatrist—and I haven't done it." We tend to look at famous people and assume they're more special than we are. But if we use Joanne Woodward's definition, there are millions of people we've never heard of who are outstanding successes. Anyone struggling to pay the rent might look at Joanne Woodward and think, "She's got it all," yet she might look at you and your accomplishments and say, "You've done it, and a lot better than I have."

All of us must develop our own personal definition of success. Mine is this: Success is feeling that if you had an unlimited amount of money, you would not change your friends, career, or lifestyle significantly.

Start with What You Don't Want

Knowing exactly what you want is rarely easy. If you are confused, start by making a list of what you know you *don't* want. Then work backwards. What you *do* want will become amazingly clear.

- If, a year from now, your life were exactly the same as it is today and you looked and felt just the same, would you throw a party to celebrate? If not, what *don't* you want that you have now?

- If the quality of your relationships—personal, romantic, professional—were identical a year from now, would you feel terrific? If not, what do you want to change?

- What if you had the same job satisfaction a year from now that you have today? Is that what you want?

- If your health and finances hadn't changed, would you be delighted? If not, what steps are you going to take *today* to make them different?

Are you starting to identify some of the things you don't want in your life? Great! That makes it much easier to identify what you *do* want. But wanting, as you may have noticed, isn't necessarily getting. You still have some important questions to ask yourself.

What Do You Want?

If the world were perfect, what would your life be like? With that ideal to guide you, make up your mind what you want and need to become the person you want to be. Unless you know what your major goals are, unless you know the difference you can make in your future or your company's future, how on earth can you set priorities?

Look to the future and decide what you want. Then acknowledge you *deserve* to get it, and believe you *will* achieve it.

Who Do You Want to Be?

Those I admire and most want to emulate are people like Dolly Parton, Cher, Oprah, and Barbara Walters, people who've decided who they want to be and then become that person. In a less showbizzy way, I've turned myself into the person I want to be.

Here's your ideal: You want to be able to say at age fifty that your life has lived up to the expectations you had when you were twenty. But that isn't quite the case with my own life. If you'd asked me, when I got off that boat from England at the age of twenty, "Patricia, draw a picture of your life thirty years from now," I absolutely could not have imagined my life today! My life has exceeded my wildest expectations. And what I do today didn't even exist then.

What Are You Willing to Give Up?

Actress Sally Field was being interviewed about her 1989 film, *Steel Magnolias*. "It was so hot," she said. "We were sweating, wearing these thick wool suits, and we were really complaining. Then I looked over at Dolly and there she was, just smiling. I said, 'Dolly, why aren't you complaining?' She told me, 'When I was young and poor, I wanted to grow up to be rich and famous. I promised myself that if ever I was, I'd never complain about anything.'"

Most people don't hope to be superstars, but they probably aspire to a certain career or lifestyle, or they say "when I marry" or "when I achieve such-and-such." Then, when they get there, all they do is complain about the inconveniences.

No job, no lifestyle, no situation comes without inconveniences and disadvantages. If you get what you asked for and grumble, you're not going to get any sympathy from me. You'll never achieve something that makes you happy if you don't start by being happy with what you've achieved. Get the life you want and then like it!

I like my life a lot. I like flying on airplanes. I like staying in hotels. I like speaking and having audiences respond to me. But if I ever started focusing on some of the inconveniences—missed flight connections, getting up at 3:00 a.m., hotel reservation foul-ups, broken sound systems, and meeting rooms much too hot or cold—and if I let these inconveniences outweigh the exciting time I spend with wonderful individuals, then I wouldn't enjoy my life as much. And you can bet if I complained about these annoyances, I would neither get, nor deserve, much pity from anyone.

That's another reason I admire Dolly Parton so much. If anyone asks her how she feels about the tabloids front-paging her private life, often inaccurately, she says, "It's part of the job. If you're not being discussed in the tabloids, people wouldn't be talking about you."

What is the life you want worth to you? Make up your mind what you are prepared to give up to reach your goal. Even highly successful people can lack balance in their lives. If your family, your physical health, and your spiritual growth are as important to you as making money, you must allow time for these things. Scheduling is only difficult when you don't know what is important to you.

What Excites You?

Trish Britt insists the dividing line between success and failure is incredibly thin. Britt is the founder of Britt & Associates, an award-winning San Francisco public relations firm. Their services include preparing people for television appearances and media interviews so they can promote their businesses, products, or projects. "It doesn't take much extra effort to succeed rather than fail," she says. As part of the preparation, Britt showers people with the questions they should be asking themselves:

- What do you like to do?

- What are your talents?
- What do you feel good about?
- What excites you?

Then Britt warns, "Be realistic about where you can start. When you have decided, really dedicate yourself to it and persist at it. No one is going to make you successful except yourself. If *you're* not trying, no one else will. If you're good at something and try very hard at it, you're going to succeed."

Joe Heitz of Heitz Cellars believes your energy should go where your passion is. He's a well-known Napa Valley personality who used to drive sixty miles to San Francisco so I could cut his hair. "People should pick something they like to do," Heitz told me. "If you like winemaking, don't try to be a banker. If you like accounting, don't ride the rodeo circuit. Get into something you enjoy. It makes work—and life—so much more pleasant."

What Are Your Power Sources?

Do you understand what motivates and drives you? Everyone has amazing sources of energy and endurance if they only know how to recognize and celebrate them.

One day, when I was in my late twenties, one of my clients told me he was about to turn fifty. "I'm throwing myself a party," he said, "but really I'm planning to celebrate for the whole year." Think about that! What a terrific way to make self-celebration a way of life any year and every year.

It's well known that it takes at least three weeks to change an ingrained habit. If you move your wastebasket from one side of your desk to the other, you'll throw paper on the floor for the next twenty-one days or so. But what if you spend the next *four* weeks, a whole month, celebrating yourself by identifying and doing the things that make you feel really good about yourself? You'd have the beginning of a habit. And if you continue doing this for the next year, imagine how it will transform your existence.

"Determine what makes you tick," says Ted Anstedt, "because this is what really helps you understand yourself and what your natural reactions are." Ted was just twenty-six when I first met him in the front row of a seminar. (I've always said that's where you meet the best people.) Since then I've watched him grow and develop into a highly successful business consultant in the banking industry and an international speaker, now based in Hillsborough, California. Ted and I got to be such chums that, when he married, I was the only woman invited to his bachelor party! I'll never forget that he drank only one glass of wine that night because, he said, he wanted to remember it.

Ted learned younger than many what his true self was. In college, he and his friends used to get together on his birthday and play Thumper, a popular drinking game with the goal of getting thoroughly drunk. To celebrate his twenty-third birthday, Ted gathered his friends, but for once they did not get drunk. Instead, he had them listen to an Earl Nightingale tape titled, "Think and Grow Rich." Afterwards, Ted asked his friends, "Now, what are we going to do with the rest of our lives? Let's start planning now." He's kept that determination:

The thing that drives me more than anything else is the desire for control over my own life and achieving a certain lifestyle, not having great wealth or power over other people. I see what happens in a lot of businesses. People go for a promotion here and a promotion there, moving all over the country, dragging their families around, and they end up struggling with frustrations, ulcers, and divorces. They're letting somebody else set their goals for them.

Earl Nightingale came up with the best definition of success I ever heard, that it's "the progressive realization of worthy ideals." You need to break up those worthy ideals into separate areas and keep track of them. The times when I've been the most unhappy with myself and with my life have been when I lost track of the balance, when I began using money as a way of keeping score.

Often in corporations, you begin to crave power. I see that a lot. I'm working with some of the world's biggest corporations—all the Fortune 500 companies. I see the people with tremendous power drives. I watch them get caught up in the game and lose sight of what their goals are. Some never had real goals in the first place. That's probably the key. I was least happy when I was unclear about my goals. You have to know yourself.

Appoint yourself the CEO of your own life! Put yourself in charge of the long-term planning, marketing strategies, promotion, fiscal policies, auditing processes, and production schedules that determine the success of your unique life venture.

Are Your Closets In Order?

Diane Parente was in the audience when I gave one of my first presentations at the Emporium in San Rafael, California. She looked so terrific that I went up to her and said, "You have to be somebody famous, but I don't recognize you."

She laughed. "I'm not famous. I'm an image consultant." I was so impressed that I walked over to the store manager and urged him to hire her for the next month's presentation, which he did on my word alone. It never occurred to me she'd never given a speech. I figured anyone who looked that good could do anything. She rose to the challenge, and now, twenty years later, the major portion of her business is corporate training and convention speaking.

I also hired Diane to reorganize my closets. She did so, both physically and metaphorically, helping me take a hard look at my priorities and ambitions. Two decades later she remains one of my best friends.

When was the last time you reorganized your clothes closets? If you say you want to look better, how about going through your wardrobe and grading everything from 1 to 10, discarding everything less than 7 (or at least putting it in a cupboard and only gardening in it).

When was the last time you reorganized the closets of your life? For instance, take a good look at the people you surround yourself with. Are they invariably supportive and eager for you to achieve what you want? Look at your habits. Will your everyday actions bring you what you want? Look at your thoughts. Do you believe in yourself? It doesn't matter what you do if, deep down, you don't think you'll attain your goals, you'll be able to do what you want to do. When you're thinking about what you want, acknowledge you *deserve* to get it. Mental closet-cleaning means getting rid of what is holding you back— any debilitating relationships, unproductive habits, or defeatist attitudes that are sabotaging you.

What Do You Need to Do?

You've now asked yourself some crucial questions. That was your first step toward deciding what you want. Your second step is to formulate specific goals. Most people think of a goal as an end that can be reached once and for all. In fact, goals are more like road plans for progressing through life. Each goal takes you part of the way, keeps you on course, and makes it harder to get lost.

Workable goals have four characteristics. They are invariably:

- challenging
- measurable
- concrete
- shared

They must be *challenging* or you'll have little motivation to try. They must be *measurable* or you won't be able to rate your progress and may not know when you've arrived. Then, to be sure they are carried out, they need to be *concrete* (written down in detail) and *shared* (co-authored, so they are supported by others).

Goals Should Be Challenging. You don't jump out of bed with enthusiasm on a Monday morning if your goal is simply to survive and make enough money to pay your lousy bills. Of course, survival can be challenging, but most people prefer to function at a higher level. On the other hand, some goals, like quadrupling your salary in the next year, may not be realistic.

This doesn't mean you will never do it, just that you might not do it next year. Goals need to be attainable as well as stimulating. So many people go to a goal-setting session or sit down with their managers to set objectives, but they make their objectives unrealistically high for the amount of energy they are prepared to put into them. Then, at year's end, they can say, "See, I told you it wouldn't work."

Goals Should Be Measurable. Be sure to keep track of your progress, so you know how you are doing. Have some sort of yardstick, not just subjective feelings that can be affected by mood swings or manipulated by outside criticism. If you are losing weight, making money, exercising—whatever it is—make sure you can measure your progress. Even people who dedicate their lives to enormous tasks—curing cancer, promoting world peace—must break their project down into measurable units.

Goals Should Be Concrete. All the things you want to accomplish should be written down. This lets you review and reaffirm them every day. Seeing your ideas in black and white helps you clarify your thinking and define your goals more clearly. What is "more"? What constitutes "better"? The simple act of writing the words and reading them back is your first concrete step toward achieving your goals.

Goals Should Be Shared. Finally, in many cases your goals will require the cooperation of those around you—your family, co-workers, or friends. At the very least, these people shouldn't hinder you. Your goals should be co-authored with the people involved. If you want to make changes in your home, organization, or community, you'll make the process more efficient when you get your colleagues to co-author your goals.

Whatever you are about to do, ask yourself, "If the world were perfect, what would this particular thing look like or be like?" Of course, the world can't be perfect, but too many times we compromise on a compromise, rather than compromising on perfection.

Choose your actions, not for how they affect today, but for where they'll get you a year or five years from now. What decisions can you make that will get you closer to the place you want to be? Remember: The unsuccessful are looking for pleasing experiences; the successful are looking for pleasing results. Have a goal. Know *where* you are going, and the *how* will follow.

FRIPPICISM

Make decisions for your tomorrows, not just your todays.

Are You Aiming High Enough?

Another of my clients, world-famous architect Gyo Obata, once said to me, "The quality of life in the world could be improved, but too many people shoot for mediocre objectives. If everyone wanted a better environment, better places to live, better places to go to school, better places to work, I think we'd have a better world." I think all of us have much more power to improve and control our lives than we realize, but we'll never find out if we aim too low.

Kit Cole encourages everyone, especially women, to expand their thinking. One thing that really burns her up is the tendency of so-called women's magazines to focus on the routines of daily life rather than helping women to aim higher. It's no wonder that, when these same magazines include surveys for their readership, the top salary box to check is $75,000/year.

Kit is a popular and successful financial advisor who does a lot of charity and philanthropic work, especially with women. Kit was twenty-seven, divorced, and had five children when she applied for a job at Dean Witter. The interviewer asked her, "How do I know you're not taking the job just to find a husband?" Kit roared with laughter. "What man in his right mind would marry a woman with five children!?" she said. That got her the job. In the early days of financial planning, Kit became part of a Dean Witter pilot program with four other women and quickly proved herself. (Although it was never her intention, she actually *did* find a husband. He also had five children, so she has raised ten.)

Can You Avoid Speed Traps?

We all know life is not simple. No matter how well we plan or how hard we work, the unexpected is always lurking, ready to zap us. At times we all get discouraged. (That's a good reason to surround ourselves with supportive people.) If you feel truly impatient about your progress over a long period, check your route for roadblocks and speed traps.

Check the Map. If things aren't happening fast enough, take a moment to examine your goals. Are they realistic? Have you mapped out logical steps to achieve them? Good things rarely come to those who just sit around and wait. Create the energy that will get you what you want. Eventually, if your plans are logical, you'll achieve success.

Check the Traffic. If your plans seem logical and your goal reasonable, check to see you're not being sidetracked by something else. Live, dream, and believe in your goals every single day. Don't spend too much time with low-priority items. Ask yourself, "What is the fastest, most efficient way to achieve my goal?" Then follow that road to the best of your ability.

Check the Destination. If you feel you are making too many sacrifices as your career progresses, perhaps you have focused on an inappropriate goal.

Do You Make Choices, Not Sacrifices?

In spite of the many years I have worked (and worked hard), I do not feel I have made too many sacrifices. I did make *choices*, however, based on what I knew was important to me. Many people have said, "Patricia, you are crazy to work as hard as you do." But for me, work—what I do—is my way of expressing myself.

No matter what you do, you must find some way in your life to express yourself at least part of the time. If you hate getting up in the morning, hate what you're doing, perhaps you should start doing something else. Maybe you'll *choose* to stay in a less-than-perfect job for now because eventually it's going to get you where you want to be. Just be sure that, in the meantime, you have at least one area of your life in which you feel fulfilled, where you can express yourself.

Are You Committed...or Just Interested?

I always say, "Tell me what you *say* you want, show me one week of your life, and I'll tell you if you'll get it." For instance, you may tell me, "I really want to get thinner." At the end of one week, have you cut out desserts? Have you started your exercise program? Have you asked a friend to commit to walking or exercising with you on a regular schedule? Have you even found out where the gyms are? If not, how would you estimate your own chances of success?

Ken Blanchard, coauthor of *The One Minute Manager*, addressing the National Speakers Association convention in San

Diego, asked, "Do you have an interest in what you say you want? Or is it a commitment? If you have an 'interest in,' you do what you have to when you feel like it or when it's convenient. But with a 'commitment to,' you never have to ask, 'Do I feel like following through today?'"

Is It a Goal or a Fantasy?

Three of my pals and I—we met at a seminar years ago—used to get together for lunch every few months to formalize our goals and check each other's progress. For his health goal, one of the cronies kept saying he wanted to trek through the Himalayas. I would reply, "I won't let you write that down as a goal. You don't even go backpacking!"

Danny Cox, one of my co-authors for *Speaking Secrets of the Masters*, says we have to know the difference between a goal and a fantasy: "With a goal you know what you can do tomorrow to get you closer to it. A fantasy is something you dream about." Both have places in our lives. Just don't confuse one with the other.

When Are You a Success?

To an extent, I can think of myself as a success today because I have achieved many of my past goals. But there is never a final goal, and you never get "there"—the place where everything is accomplished and you no longer have to worry. That's the fun of it!

I'm often glad that I didn't know when I started out what I know now. If I had, I might never have started! But even though I've worked extremely hard and experienced ups and downs, most of the time I've been exceedingly happy.

Too many people think of success as a goal to be reached once and for all, rather than a process, a way of living. A very successful New York businesswoman, Eva Stern, once said, "Don't believe you're going to open your own business and live happily ever after. That's what they used to tell us about marriage!" Eva is a wise woman. She realizes that simply achieving your goal doesn't guarantee you'll be happy—or successful. Both happiness and success are processes, ways of life. And for any entrepreneur, man or woman, success and happiness come from a succession of achievements which have been carefully planned and logically worked out. If you are not content at every step of your ladder to success, you're not going to be happy when you get there. This is something I try never to forget.

At age fifteen, I prepared for my career by cutting our neighbors' hair, rather than concentrating on dating and other standard teenage activities. I don't want to sound like a martyr—I did date—but I didn't spend a lot of time and energy out looking for fun. I used to think, "Well, when I'm a good hairstylist, then I'll have more time to play." Then it became, "When I finish my book..." or "When I've worked on this project or that project...." Now, over three decades later, I realize everything I do is fun, that I'm not postponing pleasure until I reach a goal. This is important because people never reach their goals! Before you ever get "there," you reset your goals so you can stretch and grow beyond them. You never have to worry about having a good time if you are already doing what you enjoy.

Norman Lear, the successful television producer, says, "Success is how you collect your minutes. You spend millions of minutes to reach triumph. Then you spend a thousand minutes enjoying it. If you were unhappy through those millions of minutes, what good are the thousands of minutes of triumph? Happiness is made of tiny successes, like good eye contact with your wife over breakfast. The big ones come too infrequently. If you don't have zillions of tiny successes, the big ones don't mean a thing."

Feelings of success come from the satisfaction of constant growth toward a goal you set for yourself. The older I get, the more I recognize the possibility of accomplishing practically anything in my own realm. Naturally, I can't expect to become a brain surgeon. At my age, with my lack of education, the hurdles would be too great. I also would love to sing like

Barbra Streisand, but it's not possible. However, I did have the necessary skills, energy, and ambition to develop a successful, in-demand speaking career. When you set your goals within your own abilities, you can achieve them—if you are committed.

Finally, when you get to where you want to be, look back to the beginning to remind yourself how far you've come. Enjoy this moment, and share it with cronies. If they're not as excited as you are, get new ones.

YOUR ASSIGNMENT:
Think About What You Want

FRIPPICISM

Ask yourself: "If the world were perfect, what would it look like?" Then expand your thinking to make it more so.

My First Thoughts

You may want to record your answers to questions in this book and your action plans in a journal.

Financial goals:

Physical goals:

Career goals:

Self-growth goals:

Friendship and relationship goals:

My next technology goal:

The next thing I'll commit to learn is:

Things I am willing to sacrifice to achieve my goals:

Things I am NOT willing to sacrifice to achieve my goals:

People I would like to get involved in my goals:

Ways I will reward myself as I come closer to reaching my goals:

A Five-Minute Homework Assignment

It's great to be young and have fun, but there is a time to grow up and get serious. Every day, choose one of these questions and invest five minutes thinking about it.

- What do I want to eliminate from my life?
- What do I want to add?
- How can I make my job better?
- How can I know more about my job?
- How can I advance my career?
- How can I improve my marriage or relationships?
- How can I improve me?
- What do I have to learn?

The answers may not come in a flash, but it's important to get into the habit of asking the right questions. Just five minutes a day deciding what you want, and you'll still have 1,435 minutes left to go get it.

CHAPTER 2

Taking Responsibility for Yourself

> ### FRIPPICISM
>
> *The quality of your life doesn't depend on your situation and circumstances but on how you respond to them.*

Many people like to blame their problems on others. Parents usually rank first as scapegoats, followed in later years by hostile employers and rejecting lovers. Now, most parents do the best they can, raising their children the way they were brought up themselves. They make mistakes out of ignorance rather than inflicting harm from malice. Employers and lovers also have agendas and needs that don't coincide with our own.

As adults, we become responsible for our own choices, feelings, and self-esteem. Like it or not, we are the only ones in charge of our actions and reactions. It may be very comforting to see others as the manipulators of our behavior and the source of all our woes, but this kind of thinking is a real time waster. The day that you discover you are in charge of you is the day you turn your life around. No matter what you do, no matter what happens to you, be responsible for yourself.

Dr. Leonard Zunin, author of *Contact: The First Four Minutes*, says, "The more one perceives his or her behavior and fate as dominated by friends, business associates, wife, husband, children, mother-in-law, mysterious vibrations from outer space, or circumstances beyond one's control, the greater the chance for disappointment and misfortune." Stop making excuses! Stand on your own two feet. Believe you can do it.

What Kind of World Do You Live In?

Our perceptions of the world become our world. They can brighten the dark corners or cast impenetrable gloom over the most luminous parts. The type of person you are is the type of world you live in. Your perception is your reality. To turn a popular expression around, "What you get is what you see."

How you interpret and react to problems is a strong clue to your coping style. John Coe, president of Database Marketing of Armonk, New York, divides the various approaches to problems into what he calls the "Dented Fender Philosophy." If there's a dent in the fender, you have several choices.

Responses to a Dented Fender
1. Try to find out who did it.
2. Call the insurance company.
3. Fix it.
4. Leave it and keep going.

Of course, knowing where and why the fender got dented may help you avoid future dents, but Coe's view is it doesn't matter how the fender got dented. Now that it's happened, what are you going to do about it? It's a nuisance—it's worse than a nuisance—but why spend energy being angry and upset when it's more productive to accept the problem and either fix it or go on?

Coe says, "If I find out a salesperson has been taking the company for a ride, doesn't have much paperwork to do, or doesn't make many sales, I can sit down with him or her and begin by slapping wrists. But that's like punishing a dented fender. The first thing for us to do is consider what we can do now to bring him or her up to an acceptable level. What's over with can't be changed. Learn from those things and do it better in the future.

"You know," Coe says, "my father had two opportunities in his life. One was to be a professional golfer. When he was eighteen, he beat the world-famous champion, Bobby Jones, but he decided against a golf career. The other opportunity was a chance to join the Office of Strategic Services—the famed OSS—during the war. He turned that down too. From then on, he was convinced he was a failure. And he was, because he concentrated on those two events for the rest of his life. He wasted his life walking backward into the future. Today is the only thing you can do something about."

I share Coe's sentiments. I get impatient with people who make permanent excuses out of temporary situations. If they spent as much energy being productive as they spend hanging on to their problems, they would be successful.

When you encounter a negative event, try dividing your responses into two parts:

1. Solve the problem.
2. Resolve to avoid a repeat.

Put your major energy into fixing and correcting, a *solution*. Then put minor energy into deciding what actions might prevent this problem in the future, a *resolution*.

I can easily get irritated with things that don't work, so I was very proud of myself when I followed my own advice. I live in the lowest crime area in San Francisco. One Friday, I came home, parked my car opposite my house, and ran inside to get something. I didn't lock the "Club" on the steering wheel because I expected to be back in a few minutes. But then my plans changed, and I forgot all about the car.

On Sunday, I went to get in my car. No car. I decided not to get upset. The reality of life is that, if you live in a city and your car has more than three wheels, sooner or later it's going to be stolen. My old Honda had no transportation value to anyone but me, but I've since learned they're very popular with thieves who steal them to sell the parts.

I reported the theft, and the insurance company gave me a rental car. My life was inconvenienced but not shattered. I didn't complain about the loss to anyone nor make a big deal of it. As John Coe points out, all my ranting and raving wouldn't make my car reappear, so I solved the problem, resolved to take more precautions in the future, and quickly got on with my life. That's the happy ending to my story, but there's an agreeable postscript: the car turned up intact a month later, my bright red "Club" still lying on the back seat. Some teenagers had taken it for a joyride and considerately left it in one piece.

Do you like the world you've made for yourself? I truly like mine. Even if the outcome of my car adventure had been different, being miserable and furious wouldn't have helped my Honda and would certainly have hurt me. Whatever problems come along, treat them like dented fenders and realize you have choices about how you respond.

"Shame on You"

A woman who used to work for me was mistreated by her alcoholic parents. When she was seven, her parents placed her in a foster home, where she was literally treated like a servant. She had to work from the moment she got up in the morning until she went to school, then from the time she returned until she went to bed. There was very little joy in her childhood.

At age seventeen, she cleaned a beauty school to pay her tuition there. When she graduated, she proved to be very talented and attracted many customers to her new employer's beauty shop. However, she was shy and didn't talk much about herself with her clients.

One day a very special woman sat in her chair—a woman who was able to draw out her story and who was sincerely interested in her well-being. After she had told this woman about her life, the client looked intently at her and said, "Shame on your parents for doing what they did to you! And shame on you if you let that affect your life any longer!"

Admittedly, some of us have a much better start in life than others, but nobody ever told us life was going to be fair. Life is the way it is.

For some people, being unsuccessful or ordinary seems easier because they know how that feels. It's comfortable. They maintain negative ideas about what successful people are like: hard, cold, calculating. Or, fearing responsibility, they console themselves with, "I would rather go along with the crowd than manage people who will criticize me." But you'll go crazy if you worry about what everybody else says about you. People either have the results they want in life or all the reasons for not having them.

It is never too late to make a positive start. Think about what you want to accomplish, set a plan, and take action.

FRIPPICISM

*You do what you have to do
so you can do what you want to do.*

Write Your Own Ticket

Design the lifestyle you want. A clever woman I know, Barbara, works very hard and lives frugally so she can take time off to travel and have fabulous experiences. One day she said, "Sometimes I'm embarrassed to tell people I'm just a word processor."

"No," I said, "what you are, Barbara, is someone who helps people run their businesses from time to time so you can afford to be a world traveler. Don't ever apologize for who or what you are."

At the beginning of my career as a men's hairstylist, I had the opportunity to work with the fabulous Jay Sebring, hairstylist to many movie stars and other well-known people. Although he was a brilliant publicity man and a great hairstylist, Jay was also a bit of a chauvinist. At the time, few women were in men's hairstyling, and I felt I had to work twice as hard as the men in the salon to prove to Jay that I was worth training. My efforts were not in vain, however, because Jay noticed my work.

One weekend, as he was about to fly to Los Angeles, Jay shook my hand and said, "Patricia, you are really doing great haircuts." It was tremendously exciting to have proven myself to my teacher, one of the greats in the business.

That same weekend, in Los Angeles, Jay Sebring was murdered, a victim of the Manson family massacre. I was devastated, but determined to remember everything he had tried so hard to teach me. Among other things, dealing with Jay taught me not to let male chauvinism or any other type of prejudice get in my way. Life just isn't long enough for that.

In the final analysis, we each have to succeed on our own. Today more jobs are being created by entrepreneurs than by corporations, and more women are starting those jobs. Many women entrepreneurs are concerned about their roles as women in the business world, traditionally a man's domain. They may not get much cooperation or support as they develop their businesses, but this forced independence can be a source of pride.

Truth or Dare

If you aren't honest with the rest of the world, how can you hope to be honest with yourself? Honesty isn't what you say you believe, it's what you model, encourage, reward and let happen every day.

Come with me for a moment to Oklahoma. One of my friends, proud father Bobby Lewis, was taking his two little boys to play miniature golf. "It's three bucks for you," the attendant drawled, "and three bucks for any kid who's older than six. They get in free if they're six or younger."

Bobby said, "Well, Mikey's three and Jimmy's seven, so I owe you $6.00." The attendant looked surprised. "Hey mister, do you like throwing your money away? You could have told me the big one was only six and saved three bucks. I wouldn't have known the difference."

"Yes," Bobby said, "but the kids would have known the difference."

Daring to take responsibility for your own life requires truthfulness and honesty in all your dealings, both with yourself and with others. As an individual or a company, what you do in private is as important as what you do in public.

Who Makes You Healthy?

It's very difficult to be a dynamic success when you don't feel well. When I was twenty-one, one of my beauty school teachers was an attractive, energetic woman of forty-three. We went out after class a couple of times, and over the course of the evening as she had a few drinks, I saw her face age ten years. I decided right then and there I would never drink if that's what it could do to your face in a few hours.

Anything athletic has always been against my nature. As a child, I detested field hockey and all the other games we were required to play. When I left school, I resolved I'd never again do anything even slightly athletic.

Fortunately, many of my friends took up running and bragged about how fit they had become. Somehow—and I don't know quite where it came from—I realized I wanted to be a runner to prove to myself I could do anything I set my mind to. I wanted to run. I wanted its benefits. I realized I didn't have to be a marathon runner to be healthy, but I wanted to prove to myself that I could do what I really (and realistically) desired. I wanted to do something that was unnatural for me. Now, I am completely addicted to regular exercise, have achieved half-marathons, and feel it's the best way to start the day.

Who makes you healthy? You do.

Who Makes You Wealthy?

What are you most proud of in your life? One of the things I'm most proud of is that, once I left home, I never asked my father for money. Of course, it was nice knowing he was there to bail me out if I needed it. Many people never have that luxury. But I felt my finances were now my own responsibility. I resolved never to spend money to impress other people or to live up to their idea of how a successful person should live.

FRIPPICISM

If you don't have money, don't spend it. When you have money, don't spend it all.

Remember my Honda? It might amuse you to learn I drive a 1988 Honda with 50,000 miles on it. That's because basically I'm a practical person. My Honda lives on the street in front of my house or at the San Francisco airport. I figure there's no point in buying a Mercedes for someone else to scratch.

Like most young people, I started out doing whatever my crowd wanted to do, which including skiing. I quickly discovered I don't like cold, I don't like snow, and I looked like a twit sliding down the slopes on my backside. The only good thing about the experience was telling ghost stories around the fire at night. I soon realized that, just because others want to go someplace or do something that takes time, money, and energy, if it isn't what *you* want to do, that's okay.

Who Makes You Wise?

Independence stems from a realization that we can learn to accomplish a task on our own. This can be difficult for anyone, but especially for women who have failed to acquire the confidence that comes from performing well in competitive situations. The notion that women cannot succeed on their own creeps in and sits silently in the corner until it is accepted as a given, something venerable and ultimately unassailable. The result of this acceptance shows up throughout a woman's life.

> **FRIPPICISM**
>
> *When you find someone who knows something you want to know, don't be shy. Ask!*

While helping to coach the women's basketball team at the college where he taught, Dick Friedrich, professor of English, observed this phenomenon. "It was fascinating for me to see how the psychological and physical oppression of women takes place. We can see how they practice what they have been taught about athletics and excellence in competition. A good deal of what men have been taught about themselves, how they can get better, and how they can learn, just hasn't been a part of the women's education. It has been enough that women could play basketball without breaking their fingers—they have not been expected to do well, to excel. It's been enough for them to play at all.

"Women haven't been taught to pretend they 'know it all,' as men have. When you try to teach women something, if you can get them to practice it through their initial expected failures, they learn it. They do progress, and it's fun to watch."

Who makes you wise? You do.

Who Makes You Happy?

Both men and women today recognize that our society used to program most women to believe their fulfillment depended on how well they satisfied others. This usually meant marriage and motherhood. Fortunately, to their delight or sorrow, many women discovered this was not necessarily true. Whatever your sex, before you make others responsible for your happiness and fulfillment, consider this. You are going to continue to grow all your life. If you feel you must have marriage, a "relationship," or children to be fulfilled, ask yourself, "With all the enormous possibilities that lie ahead of me, do I still want to commit to this now? Will this step make me more productive and open to growth?"

If your answer is "yes," your next question should be "What compromises am I prepared to make and continue to make?" I feel fortunate indeed that my mother brought me up to think that marriage is great (my parents were happily married for forty-five years), but not essential. She never programmed me to think I would be unsuccessful if I did not marry. Paradoxically, today's mothers often have the opposite challenge: not to convey that their daughters are "giving up" their futures if they choose to have husbands and children!

More than ever, being your own person and having your own career can make life easier in the long run. This applies, of course, to both men and women. I feel deeply for people who suddenly, through a spouse's death or departure, or their own feelings, wake up alone believing they have no choices. There is an aching irony here. So many people get married because they are afraid to be alone, but divorce statistics show marriage is not a guarantee you will have company and support when you grow older. *Learn to fend for yourself.* Have something you do well— something that makes you feel good, that gives you self-esteem. Then you can handle a lot of other problems.

But some women, psychologist Dru Scott Decker notes, continue to have difficulties thinking about what they want for themselves. These are the women who, after many years of feeling caught between the "husband first" and "children first" schools of thought, still need outside permission to want something for themselves.

Let me give you permission: It's quite all right to want anything in the world as long as it doesn't hurt someone else. Any relationship is doomed unless people are together because they choose to be, each benefiting and growing from the alliance. If you're marrying or having an ongoing affair with someone just to have someone else in the room while you read the paper, you're doing two people a grave disservice.

All of us should have something exciting and fulfilling in our lives that doesn't require the presence of our nearest and dearest. Such activities send us back to our loved ones refreshed and interesting. It's a classic Catch-22 situation: Only when you take responsibility for your own happiness and fulfillment will you find it in your relationships.

Who makes you happy? You do.

"I Can Do That!"

One of my best friends, Shirley Davalos, made an opportunity for herself and then panicked and said "no." It took her five hard years before she made the same opportunity a second time.

When Shirley got out of college, she wanted to get into television. Everyone told her to start in a small town, but she went straight to a "major market," San Francisco. There she got an interview at a local radio station and was offered a job—as a producer!

Shirley gulped. "What would the job entail?"

She was told she'd be responsible for calling important people like the mayor and asking them to appear on the show. "For instance, if the mayor is involved in a breaking news story, you'll call her up and ask her to be on the show the next day."

"I couldn't do that," Shirley said. "I've never done it before. I don't know how. Couldn't I start with something lower?" Her potential employer showed her the door. It was five years before Shirley broke into television.

During those five years she worked in several banks, still going for interviews at radio and television stations. She finally got a job as receptionist at KBHK-TV, a local station. Once in the door, she went to every department offering her services. "I'm just sitting here most of the time," she'd say. "Is there anything I can be doing to help you?" She quickly became a production assistant, making the same kind of phone calls that had panicked her five years earlier. She also started writing the movie vignettes for the newspaper TV listings.

Now that Shirley knew people in the business, she learned about a production secretary job at KGO-TV, an ABC affiliate. It was only for three months, replacing a woman on maternity leave, but Shirley decided to risk it. She survived the three months and stayed on with KGO-TV, eventually becoming a production secretary on the morning program "A.M. San Francisco." As the program grew in importance, Shirley did too, becoming its producer three years later.

Eventually, Shirley decided to take another big step and start her own company, Orion Express Television Production/ Media Services. The California firm has produced and developed television programs airing nationally on channels like PBS, CNBC, and the Discovery Channel as well as promotional programs for business and corporate clients.

Shirley Davalos has brought herself a long way from the shy young woman who missed a big opportunity because she didn't think she had the nerve to telephone the mayor. Shirley has three pieces of advice for others:

1. *Ask, "How can I help you?"* Start anywhere, then make yourself indispensable.

2. *Don't be in love with a title.* Be in love with your work. Many people choose a job they think is going to be

glamorous, that will do this or that for them, but they're looking for ego, not work.

3. *Persevere.* That's how I got into television. My father said, "The last key on the ring that opens the door is perseverance. You may notice other people getting lucky breaks or undeserved success, but if you just keep working at it, things are going to happen for *you.*"

Shirley Davalos could have spent the rest of her life recalling how luck had been against her or how she had blown her one lucky break. Instead, she made herself responsible for her own life. She made herself indispensable, ignored job titles, and persevered until she got inside the door and got the job she wanted.

The Dancing Cowboy

You can gauge how far you've come in life by your reaction to this poem by my friend Carolyn Long.

Across the floor the cowboy strode
With sure and steady grace,
In boots of tan and coat of hide,
As a slow smile warmed his face.

Showing teeth like pearls in a face so fine
You could almost hear hearts break.
His eyes made me fear I'd less likely drown
If I fell in a deep blue lake.

His hat, it seemed, brushed the lower beams;
He held every eye entranced,
But the Cowboy had eyes for only one.
My heart leapt as he advanced.

The band played "Achy Breaky Heart"
And mine was well at risk.
His eyes invited me to dance
Like we'd planned a secret tryst.

I have danced, it's true, most all my life,
But never like this before:
From the moment he took my hand in his
My feet never touched the floor.

"Look deep in my eyes," the Cowboy said,
"And you'll know just what to do."
They led me to laugh and to cry and to sing
And to dance every dream I knew.

We danced and we whirled all around the room
In moves I'd never seen.
But I followed every step he took
Like a well-rehearsed routine.

I couldn't help smiling and dancing with joy
Like a little kid just having fun!
We two-stepped and waltzed and his eyes danced with mine
And we looked to the world like one.

It was hard to imagine life anywhere else
Or that we'd ever be apart,
"A cowboy looks at teeth," he said,
"And your smile stole my heart."

Now some women seek, some just wait;
Some pray while others scheme.
But single or wed or young or old,
Each harbors a secret dream

Of dancing nights on smooth oak floors
'Til the room is just a blur
With a handsome, dancing tall cowboy
Whose eyes are just for her.

The Cowboy never stays for long;
One kiss and then he's gone.
But he'll fill enough of a woman's dreams
To last a lifetime long.

©1993

I believe the quality of our lives depends on how we respond to the circumstances and situations we find ourselves in. You can look at Carolyn's poem as "What an adventure!" Or you can say, "Hey, the bum left in the end!"

YOUR ASSIGNMENT:
Dented Fender Incidents in My Life

> **FRIPPICISM**
>
> *Appoint yourself Chairman of the Board of your own life.*

1. What dented fender incidents am I still wasting energy on?

2. What is the first thing I am going to let go of?

3. What is my first step to do this?

4. How will I reward myself when I have done this?

A Thirty-Second Homework Assignment

Take half a minute each morning as you look in the mirror to complete the following sentence. "As President and CEO of my own life, today I am totally responsible for..."

CHAPTER 3

Coping With and Creating Change

FRIPPICISM
Never argue with the inevitable.

No one is a stranger to change. It visits us daily. Its challenge is so consuming of our daily lives that few have the luxury of contemplating its size or speed.

Here are three ways to deal with change.

- *Accept* that everything, both good and bad, will change, and you'll usually be able to find something useful, good, and healthful in the new situation.

- *Participate* actively in the inevitable changes in your personal life, your company, your organization, and your company. Act, don't re-act from necessity, letting events and other people dictate your life.

- *Believe* strongly that your actions influence the outcome. *You* can make a difference.

Hope and optimism are terrific, especially when they're based on the reality of where life is now. We are living in a downsized, re-engineered, outsourced world. That is our reality.

Lots of people who worked hard for the same company for twenty-five years have suddenly gotten laid off at age fifty. No, it's not fair, but that's life. No matter what you do or where you work, you need to become Chairman of the Board of your own life. I certainly advocate being loyal to your employer, not only because it's good for your career, but because it's the right thing to do. However, your goal is to be *employable*, not just employed. While you're being loyal and dependable, be sure you're visible in your company, your community, and your industry. Then, if (or when) you are laid off, the word goes out, "Oh, good, a wonderful person is available." The only security in life is your self-confidence that you can adapt and *change*, that you're versatile and flexible enough to go in another direction.

Taking Risks

In *Risking*, David Viscott says:

If your life is ever going to be better, you have to take risks. There is simply no way you can grow without doing so. It is surprising how little most people know about taking risks. Often people become inhibited by the fear that, any moment, they must commit themselves to action. At the first sign of reversal, they damn themselves and hesitate, feeling that the situation is about to fall apart. Then they retreat untested, protesting they were in over their heads and thankful to escape. They do not understand that to risk is to exceed one's usual limits. The uncertainty and danger are simply a part of the process.

Viscott adds, "We hold onto bad habits because we are not really committed to growing. We need an excuse for our failures. We keep our bad habits because we do not really love ourselves."

People find it difficult to abandon any investment—in money, love, time, effort, or commitment. Sometimes we outgrow certain investments. When that happens, we shouldn't consider our previous expenditures a waste. These were the things that made us who we are today, so they were well worth it.

Other times, we notice some investments have become unproductive or even harmful. These are best abandoned. As Max Gunther relates in *The Luck Factor*, "A Swiss banker, a self-made millionaire, summed up his investment philosophy thus: 'If you are losing a tug of war with the tiger, give him the rope before he gets your arm. You can always buy a new rope.'"

Big Changes in the Workplace

Recent changes in the life of my friend Marie Randall led her to discover what she calls "a major value-shift" among many successful American businesswomen—changes that may affect how the upcoming generation think about their working lives.

"When I was a child," says Marie, "there was no doubt in our household that education was essential, that I would go on to earn bachelor's and master's degrees, maybe even a Ph.D. My expectation—or illusion—was I'd become one of these multi-dimensional women with a promising career and a family. I bought into what I now call the Super Woman Ideal.

When Marie graduated from Michigan State University with a Bachelor's degree in psychology, she was accepted for a Master's program. However, she arranged to take a short break first. Then she got involved in a highly successful sales career. Recently, at age thirty-nine, she decided to go back to school.

Given her busy and successful career, I simply had to ask Marie why she felt she needed another degree. "Actually," she explained, "my original bachelor's degree in psychology was a marvelous background for sales. In terms of understanding people and motivation, especially in business, it's been indispensable. But now I'm at a point in my career where I either continue in the same direction or go into management. At forty,

I'm going through some reassessments, and part of that is realizing there is potential burnout in what I'm currently doing. Fortunately, selling is a transferable skill. I could transition to a different industry, but instead I want to take my knowledge and use it in a different application. With a master's degree, I can do that."

The changes in Marie Randall's own life inspired her choice of subject for her master's thesis: "Catching Their Balance: Baby-boomer Businesswomen Encounter a New Type of Mid-life Crisis."

Of these changes, Marie says, "My own reassessment, rethinking, redefining success, and encompassing a new sort of self-image—they were all motivators for researching this topic. Not only does it reflect personal soul searching but also the angst of my friends and colleagues. It was something women wouldn't discuss openly because to do so would hint they no longer believed in the Super Woman Ideal. But then the media began highlighting it, which provided a fertile source of recent statistics."

Today's businesses, says Marie, are discovering that many of the trailblazing women who are at the pinnacle of their success are beginning to blaze new trails right *out* of the corporate milieu. These are the women who poured into the work force in the 1970's and were groomed for years to take over. Instead, they're leaving.

Why are they making this transition? Marie feels their departure reflects "a schism between the internal and external personae that women in this particular group are experiencing." In other words, these women have been fulfilling their professional needs at the expense of their personal needs. Now they want to try something new. "Once they reached this place," Marie says, "all of a sudden there's this big question, 'Is that all there is? Something is missing. I want more.'"

"A relationship with a man is important, but only as part of a whole. Your self-worth and self-image depend on your beliefs and value systems, on your core self." Elsa Ward, in her book *Divided Life*, tried to come up with a way to measure a woman's well-being. She initially decided the defining areas for women were work, relationships with men, and relationships with children. Then she added three more: time to oneself, time with others (one's support system), and a sense of place or home. But, as Ward continued her research and interviews, she decided there was a seventh measure of well-being that overshadowed all the others. It was a woman's sense of autonomy, independence, and self-image. Ward found that a woman's self-definition either bolstered or negated the other six areas. In other words, much of life is a balancing act.

Marie Randall addresses this need for balance in her four tips for dealing with changing times and changing lifestyles.

1. Strive for balance. Compromise. Objective perfectionism can't be achieved in every single aspect of your life.

2. Get in a supportive environment of people who understand "success" is self-defined and there are many ways to be successful.

3. Think of yourself as an entrepreneur, whatever you do. This empowers you, gives you transferable skills, and gets you out of the box.

4. Help the next generation realize we have to be open to talking and thinking about alternatives for dealing with female employees so we can get their wonderful input.

Whose Problem Is It?

"One of my employees was driving me nuts," says JR Parrish, currently Chairman of Colliers USA, and owner of three real estate offices. Years ago, when JR was with the Producers' Dairy in Fresno, he learned a life-altering lesson. "I had a milkman who had been with the company for about twenty years, a real fixture, but he had an alcohol problem. He was a relief driver, but at least once a week he wouldn't show up. Then I'd get a phone call at 2:00 a.m. and have to get out of bed and go do that route myself.

"One day I told Glen Lay, creator of the 'Better World Theory', that this guy was driving me out of the business. I hated covering for him. Glen told me something that changed my whole perspective. 'This is not this man's problem,' he said. 'This is *your* problem.' I was incredulous.

"'How can it possibly be *my* problem?' I thought. Then I understood he was right. In the 'Better World Theory,' if something is wrong in your life, it's not your mother's problem or your father's problem, or the fault of the government or your employer. A better world starts with *you*. If you want change, you have to cause the change. I couldn't make this man change his life. I could only change the situation."

The Scandal of the Red Undies

Coreen Cordova is a very flamboyant woman with lots of flair. Diane Parente first introduced me to her through Women Entrepreneurs in 1977. At that point, Coreen had the contract to do all the makeups within a facial salon that offered other services. When Coreen decided it was time to make a change and get her own makeup studio, she spoke to a friend, Kit Cole, who was one of the first female stockbrokers. "How can I go into business for myself?" Coreen asked. "I have no start-up money."

"Not a problem," Kit said. A week later, Kit called and reported, "You've got $25,000. Five women have each lent you $5,000. Now go and get your own space. Open your business!"

Coreen became the best-known makeup artist in San Francisco, with most of the TV celebrities and society people coming to her for advice. Soon she was a regular on the local TV show, "People Are Talking." Coreen is very attractive and vivacious, but she let the audience know she was much like them, with some of the same insecurities and imperfections. She would often go on camera with only half her face made up so she could show the audience a "before" and "after."

In the early 1990s, a headhunter telephoned Diane Parente and described an exciting job opportunity. "Are you the person we're looking for?"

"No," Diane told them, "You want Coreen Cordova."

The job was with Amway, a large direct-sales company. They wanted someone to help Amway distributors sell their "Artistry" beauty products line. Coreen started doing weekend presentations on a contract basis. After the first year, Amway was so thrilled with what she did that they offered her full-time employment.

Another major career change. Coreen decided to close her salon and went full-time with Amway. But her first important event was nearly her last. "I wasn't really familiar with their background or who their distributors were and what Amway is all about. I failed miserably.

"I thought they'd hired me to impress everyone with how fabulous the products are, and the way to do this was to be incredibly impressive myself. So I wore my most gorgeous suit. My hair and makeup were absolutely perfect. I must have gone over my script a million times. Then I got up in front of this group and, boy, did I dazzle them. But they all just sat there, arms crossed, legs crossed. I bombed."

Several women were so incensed, they complained to the president and the head of marketing: "We don't like her. We don't want her here!" When asked why, they reported, "She said 'underwear' and she said 'Jane Fonda.'"

"Well, yes, I had," Coreen admits. "I'd mentioned Jane Fonda, whom they consider too politically outspoken and not properly respectful of men. And I told them I like to wear red on television because it energizes me and gives me a more powerful personality. 'I even wear red underwear,' I said. Well, you just don't say things like this in front of Amway people. Then, as they were still reeling, I mentioned I used to be a 'winter' with black hair so I always wore winter colors, but now I'd become an 'autumn' or 'spring.' That really threw them because they don't believe you can alter your coloring. The whole audience was in shock: 'This is going to be our new leader? Look at her!'

"To succeed with Amway, I had to take a hundred steps backwards and start over. Fortunately, I got the chance to change, to reinvent myself so I was the person they wanted to deal with. I'd shown them what I thought they wanted— sophistication and being smart about beauty. But what they really wanted was a girlfriend, not a flashy know-it-all facade. They wanted a friend at the top who could tell them the secret of how to do this or that, someone to laugh with and joke with. They wanted somebody who could touch them and empower them, but in their own way. They wanted to feel wonderful about themselves, but not superior to the men in their lives."

Coreen's chance to adapt came through confrontation with her critics. "The marketing people asked me to meet with a few of the distributors who were most against me," she recalls. "I was scared to death because I had hoped this would be a great change in my career and now it might be over." Fortunately for Coreen, she went in with her defenses down, ready to learn where she had gone wrong. The distributors were prepared to tell her, too. "The ladies explained, 'What we really want to know is who you are. We didn't hear that.'" The Amway distributors who had been her audience were actually more accepting of her as an individual than anybody she had previously worked with. Her subsequent experiences with Amway have been personally uplifting as well as professionally successful. She is now their spokesperson. "I go around making the line look good and developing new products. I've put together a merchandising system that's making them an extra $3 million or $4 million a month. That's why the company does so much for me—because I deserve it and because I give them who I am.

"It's still like owning my own business. I have to reinvent myself every day. Even when you have a business for twenty years as I did, you can't just walk through it. Every day you have to reinvent who you are, you have to make it exciting again, you have to do it over, come up with new ideas, new techniques. It's being open to change. It's taking something good and making it better and better."

> FRIPPICISM
>
> *Your goal is not to be employed, but to be employable in this changing world.*

When You're Not Wanted

"Change is sometimes forced upon you," says Susan RoAne. She is a former schoolteacher who made a big career jump when she got laid off. Happily, she landed on her feet, becoming a journalist, popular lecturer, and best-selling author, but it wasn't easy.

Her first decision was to change careers. "When I was first laid off," RoAne says, "I decided any profession that didn't want me didn't deserve me." She began looking around and checking want ads. At a networking seminar, RoAne met Sally Livingston. "Sally became my mentor—my *femme-tor* as she used to say. Through her I networked with terrific people like Betty Lehan Harragan, who wrote *Games Your Mother Never Taught You*, and Jane Trahey, who wrote *On Women and Power*. My life really changed."

One of the first things RoAne did was to design career-changing workshops for other teachers, charging just five dollars a participant. To promote the workshops, RoAne sent brochures to teachers and school districts. Hoping for more publicity, she telephoned Bea Pixa at the *San Francisco Examiner*. "You may not remember me," RoAne said, "but you once spoke for my class." Pixa replied, "I remember you very clearly because yours was the only class in my ten years of speaking that sent me thank-you notes." Pixa wrote an article about RoAne that filled the workshops.

Then, when RoAne was on a local radio show to talk about career changes, the business editor of the *San Francisco Examiner* called and asked her to do a column. For years she had taught writing to her students and written letters her friends found "fabulously funny," so she decided to give it a try. She ended up designing and writing a career series for the *Examiner* for the next three years. "At first, I'd complain to friends that I hated sitting all day to write that column. Then I realized it was much better to be writing *for* a paper than grading one."

One day she attended a seminar by Judith Briles on getting published. Briles held up an *Examiner* article that RoAne had brought, "How to Work a Room."

"Sue, you can really write!" Briles said. "This should be a book. Here's the name of my agent."

Twenty-one turndowns later, she found a publisher. The book has now sold well over a million books in eight countries and nearly a decade later is still selling. Since then she's written two more books, *The Secrets of Savvy Networking* and *What Do I Say Next?*

I asked Susan RoAne what advice she'd give to people in career transition, forced or otherwise. "Sit down and make two lists," RoAne says.

- *Assess your skills.* "Most people in transition have no clue how much they do well because nobody has ever told them. They take whatever they do for granted because it's their skill, much like I take writing for granted because it's my skill: 'Oh, it's easy, you just pick up a pen.' For most people, it's not that easy. My friend who makes great apple pie once told me making pie crust is easy. And I replied, 'Only because you know how to do it. For me, it's complicated.'"

- *Assess your interests.* "Decide what you like to do best. If you don't like organizing, even if you're good at it, make sure your next job doesn't require it. If you're good at cold calling but don't like to do it, don't."

"Now get some crayons," RoAne says. ("We teachers are great on crayons, but colored pens will do.) Circle the things you like to do in green, and circle the things you do the most in red. See if there is any overlap. Green is where your power is. Your goal is to find work in which most of what you do has both a red and a green circle around it.

"Change is sometimes forced upon you. I would not have left teaching voluntarily. I loved it, and I was good at it. You control your own classroom. You can be bossy. And people thank you. Or sometimes they don't. Sometimes the messages come, not from what you *want* to do, but from what you are *forced* to do. And you had better be ready to rise to the occasion."

Out on the Street

Do you know someone who has literally gone from affluence and influence to food stamps and then rebuilt her life? I do.

Judith Morgan Jennings was a TV publicist, first in Cleveland and then in San Francisco, where she also had a talk show on KGO radio. But when her ten-year marriage to a KGO-TV anchor broke up, her successful career ended abruptly.

"I didn't think it was a bad marriage. I knew no one 'has it all,' and I certainly didn't, but not many of my friends did, either. I assumed having a workable, doable relationship was all anyone could ask. Then all of a sudden it became clear it wasn't enough, and there was no point in going on.

"I left my husband on a Tuesday, and I was let go from my radio job two days later. It made sense. In the 1970s it was unusual for a woman to leave a man, certainly not a man in a highly visible position. My husband was Number One and I was number nothing. He was the talent and I was a convenience. I had suspected this was a possibility, but I hadn't thought it through entirely. My husband was so upset that he didn't want me in the building. In fact, years later, when I came back as a publicist, he required twenty-four hours notice if I was going to be in the building so he wouldn't run into me.

"I looked for work, tailoring my resume for all kinds of things, but it took five months to land another job. In the meantime, the small amount I could collect from unemployment insurance ran out. I had walked away from the marriage without asking for anything, so I had to apply for food stamps. I was thirty-six years old, and, for a woman in television, that's ancient. I was certainly one of the oldest in the industry that I knew about.

"Food stamps were a very humbling ordeal. First of all, establishing eligibility is a tortuous process designed to defeat all but the brightest and most dedicated. They're not 'free' unless you are totally indigent—you can pay up to 90 percent of face value for them. Then even using them can be a challenge. I'd done talk shows where people denounced food stamp recipients for driving off in their Cadillacs or using the stamps to buy caviar and champagne. The reality is quite different. You're not allowed to buy anything not grown in the U.S. nor alcoholic beverages—no coffee, no bananas, and definitely no caviar. Not even toilet paper and soap. I certainly became a better, wiser talk show host for the experience.

"There was no such thing as networking then, and few people would accept my calls, interview me, or refer me. When I finally did get in the door, I was usually interviewed by a twenty-six year old male with his feet up on the desk. It wasn't pleasant. I vowed then and there that when I was back on my feet, I'd talk to everyone, and I kept that promise.

"During this time, I got rid of a lot of physical and mental clutter in my life. When you're that far down, there are very few choices. Most things are 'yes' or 'no' without any gray areas. This requires a lot of discipline, but it's liberating, not to be surrounded by things. I really like what I've become as a result of this experience. I can't honestly say I'd be the person I am if it had never happened."

Judith reestablished her career as a publicist, stronger than ever, and went on to win a long list of industry awards. "They're lots of fun to hang on the wall," she notes, "and on days when the rug has been pulled and you've lots of doubts, it's nice to go over and look at them. Sometimes you need outside support systems."

Part two of Judith's life contains the happily-ever-after. Though immediate remarriage wasn't in her plans, she soon fell in love with an extraordinary man and started over. At first they both struggled economically—"not nearly as romantic as some of the books I've read"—but a therapist friend asked her if she'd rather have waited another twenty years before meeting him. "A light went on," says Judith, "and I realized I was so fortunate to have met him when I did. We've been married for over twenty years."

Judith is still going through growth experiences and changes. Recently, her older husband decided to retire. Judith, in her late fifties, chose to start over with a new job for Fox Communications in San Diego so she could commute to their dream home in Mexico. "I still don't know what next year will bring," she says. "I look at it as a journey, and I pay attention to the signs out there and the silence between thoughts, making sure I'm tapping all the resources."

Creating Your Own Change

I have always had a great faith in life—that things work out the way they are supposed to. I believe we have choices. I believe we set goals and design our lives, that we create change as well as react to it. I believe there is a certain order to the universe; I believe there are few accidents.

I've also had faith I'll get everything in my life when it's the right time for me to have it. Even so, all my opportunities have come in ways that never let me relax. I've had to keep learning and growing and getting ready—and then the opportunity has come.

Activity gets results, though it isn't always possible to relate a specific action to a specific outcome. For example, if I do a mass mailing and a few days later the phones start ringing, it isn't necessarily the people who just got the flyer who are calling. The calls may come from people I contacted a year or two before. Continual output brings continual outcomes.

Some changes in my life have been difficult, and I have had a few traumas, but I've always felt there was a reason for them. The people in my life mean something to me. I hope and trust I am playing as important a part in their lives as they are in mine. I would not for a moment suggest that anyone believe exactly what I believe. I encourage people to think and read and research alternatives so they can make up their minds for themselves. You can't change the world, but you can change yourself, and if you change yourself, suddenly you find the world has changed.

YOUR ASSIGNMENT:
Coping with and Creating Change

FRIPPICISM

Change:
always inevitable,
often good and healthful,
rarely without some redeeming
opportunity.

1. What has been the best change in my life?

2. Why was it the best?

3. What did I learn?

4. How did people around me respond to this change?

5. What positive things did I learn from this change?

6. What has been the most difficult change for me to accept?

7. What fears about this change were unfounded?

8. What good things have come out of this change?

9. How will I feel about change in the future?

10. What is the dumbest thing I ever did that I learned something from?

11. Could I have avoided this change?

12. How can I seek the benefit in this change?

13. What will I do so I feel more comfortable about change?

14. Will I be one of the people in my industry who helps to manage and guide change?

15. Am I confident I can handle the changes the future will inevitably bring?

Are you surprised at your answers?

A Homework Assignment

List at least five changes you anticipate will occur in your life during the next five years. Are they positive or negative? Are you ready for them? (Positive changes can be as stressful as negative ones!) What can you do now to prepare?

CHAPTER 4

Cracking Your Comfort Barrier

FRIPPICISM
Our aim shouldn't be to have an easy life, but to have a better quality of problems.
Robert Fripp

If you're going to adapt to the frequent changes that bombard us, you're going to have to push past your comfort zone. Change, even good change, makes us uncomfortable. That's why we so often stick with old, unproductive habits, rather than trying something new.

Adapting to change is going to make you feel uneasy, distressed, even miserable. This discomfort is absolutely necessary before you can become the person you want to be. If you are going to make a difference in your company or your country, you are signing on for some discomfort.

It's okay to feel uncomfortable. If you think back on the most successful times in your life and how you felt before that success, you'll realize you were darned uncomfortable. That's because you were walking on new ground.

What's the Best Defense?

Knowing what you want is the key to avoiding discomfort by adapting successfully to new situations. When you know where you are going, you can handle the rough spots as you adapt and set up your future. Some of the best decisions I've made in my life—leaving England to come to America, opening a business, investing in real estate, becoming a public speaker—were terrifying at the time, but having these clear goals made the changes much less difficult.

When I was waving goodbye to my mother, I had no idea when we would see each other again. I told her not to cry because I knew if she did, I would. My father kept asking, "How do you know it will be better? What if you don't get a job? You won't be able to call your mother every day." He wasn't discouraging me as much as he was making sure I realized what I was doing.

Years later, my mother confided he had said, "Tell her not to go," but she had refused. Now, when I look back at myself at twenty, I understand why he did that. I'm amazed I made it. I wasn't very sophisticated; I had no idea what I was doing. But one reason youth succeeds is that we have no idea what can go wrong.

Things were nice for me in England. I enjoyed home. I had a good job. I had a nice boyfriend and lots of friends. I was comfortable. But something in me insisted I go exploring. I was *uncomfortable* leaving, but I knew it was what I had to do.

Handling the Discomfort

People don't always see you the way you see yourself. When I was on the same program with Patty Duke, I was astonished to discover that this fine actress was petrified of speaking in public. After her presentation, she answered questions from the audience. That seemed much more comfortable for her. I asked her, "What is the toughest part about being president of the Screen Actors' Guild?" I loved her answer.

"The title. Any title can be intimidating. You have to look past it to the person who held the position before. When you realize he or she was a human being, then you say, 'Hey, I can do it too.'"

Achieving success—*your* success on *your* terms—is not a painless process, but it's worth it. To follow through on our resolves for change, we need to get out of our comfort zone. Any success I've achieved has nothing to do with being brilliant or well-educated. I'm neither. For me it was a struggle to be fifteenth in a class of thirty, but I always turned up and I developed good work habits. I got out and educated myself with people, books, situations. Any secrets to success aren't secrets, because there are people who will teach them to you. I'll tell you the "secrets" of my success. They were tenacity, working a little harder, and the willingness to crack my comfort barrier.

In a time management seminar, I once asked the participants why they were there. One woman said, "Well, I am successful, but I'm comfortable. I want to learn how to get uncomfortable so I can be even more successful."

Stretching Yourself

In 1975 I started demonstrating haircuts. Three snips into my first public demonstration I cut a big hole in my finger. Blood was oozing, but I finished the haircut. I had to keep stopping to mop my finger with a towel. Fortunately, my model had black hair! At other times I have cut hair in front of people who were totally unimpressed. I didn't like those feelings of failure and rejection and embarrassment. But I got up again and again and again until I made it worthwhile for those watching— and worthwhile for myself.

At the beginning of my speaking career, I always sought out the most difficult situations in which to stretch and grow. I have spoken in San Bruno Prison to female inmates and in San Quentin; I have spoken to 150 hearing-impaired people through a signing interpreter, and to 150 ten- to twelve-year-olds which was hard because you never get their attention all at once, and they all have different ideas of what is funny. The toughest crowd was 9,000 teenagers—not because there were 9,000 of them but because they were teenagers. One of my friends who accompanied me to this program thought it was a good experience for me because, as he said, "You're getting too used to people telling you you're good." That day I promised myself to accept any assignment that would help me grow as a person and as a speaker.

So often, once we reach a competence level in our careers, we are happy to coast. Many of the most dissatisfied people have accomplished major goals and then don't look for more opportunities. Grab any opportunity to develop beyond your present comfort barrier. When that old "too comfortable" feeling creeps up on me, I get suspicious. It makes me scrutinize my life.

FRIPPICISM

If you focus on what could go wrong, it gets in the way of what can go right.

Painful Mistakes

One of the biggest reasons people are not successful is they procrastinate. And one of the biggest reasons people procrastinate is they dread the discomfort of making mistakes.

But here's the news: The only people who don't make mistakes are those who don't attempt anything. Often the worst mistake you can make is not doing something—anything! Sitting tight because you are afraid to move is as pointless as racing about just to be doing something.

Waiting...and Waiting

A woman came up to me after a speech I gave about "Decisions That Can Turn Your Life Around." She said, "I realize I have been putting off things since my husband died. I was waiting until I lost weight and until this occurred or that happened."

Reasons for waiting always seem to make sense at the time, but they are just excuses. Soon waiting becomes a bad habit, a way of life.

Psychologist Dru Scott Decker talks about what she calls the "for best" syndrome—how, when she was a child, her family's silver was always kept "for best." It was too good for Friday night's Kentucky Fried Chicken or Wednesday night's spaghetti. Her father died, and then her mother had a stroke, and Dru looked after her. Though it was a struggle for her to talk, Dru's mother took her hand one day and said, "Take out the best silver. 'For best' is now."

People are always waiting. "I won't buy new clothes or try to meet new people until I lose weight," they decide, or "I won't do this until the children go to school," "I won't start that until the children have left home," or "I won't do this until I get a divorce" (or "until I get married"). If there's something you really want to do, *do it now*!

Discipline vs. Procrastination

Setting goals, having ideas, and knowing what you want is just the beginning. What counts is having the ongoing consistency, the dedication, and the *discipline* to make it happen.

Danny Cox, one of my co-authors in *Speaking Secrets of the Masters*, says, "Every year on January 1, I set a theme for the coming year." What a great idea, I thought. Soon after, I had a chance to put it to work in my own life.

I was spending Christmas at a health spa in Palm Springs. I've found it's the one time I can be sure to get away and totally take my mind off business. As I relax, exercise, and work on projects, I begin to think anything in the world is possible. One morning, I pulled out a tee-shirt my brother had given me. He had recorded an album called "Discipline" and had lots of shirts printed with the album's logo. On the back they said, "Discipline, not an end in itself but a means to an end." But that morning, I discovered a different slogan: "Discipline: a vehicle for joy."

What a wonderful concept. Think of all the negative words people associate with *discipline*: severity, discomfort, harshness, rigor, penalty, even punishment! Why not replace them with an image of a bright, shiny vehicle, sweeping you past all the sidetracking temptations toward your real joy. I decided to follow Danny Cox's example and make my brother's maxim my theme for the year.

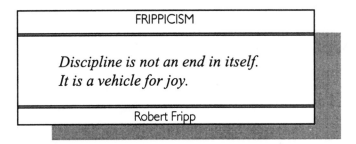

FRIPPICISM

Discipline is not an end in itself.
It is a vehicle for joy.

Robert Fripp

The Discipline of Having the Best

When you say "no" to yourself or someone else, "no" to this choice or that, it's discipline. Years ago I had an important business decision to make, and I was worried about making the "right" one. A friend, Wendy, told me something that has made decision-making easier ever since. She said, "Patricia, with the energy and enthusiasm you put into everything you do, you will make either choice a success."

If you have sixteen things you can do, start by analyzing the pros and cons on paper, and then go with the one that feels right, the one that will bring you and the world closer to perfection. You might even ask yourself, "if the world were perfect and money not a consideration, what would I do?" Of course, money *is* a consideration, but when you are making decisions, it clouds your judgment. If you are trying to choose between two outfits and one is on sale for half price, would that affect which you choose? It shouldn't. I'm going to tell you something that your mother never did: Don't look at the price tag! If the outfit that makes you feel like a million dollars isn't on sale, put it on layaway.

Sometimes there's something you can't afford right away, but once you have the idea, you can adapt and plan for it. Just expand your thinking. We're so programmed to think, "I can't afford it so I'll settle for second best." I say, "If you can't afford it, wait and have the best."

Catching the Bus

Each of us needs to work hard and feel uncomfortable sometimes. My father, Arthur Fripp, said, "Some people catch the bus and some don't. You have a better chance of going places if you're in the waiting zone when the bus arrives."

If you don't go out and do things, you'll remain forever fearful of the workings of the world. Go out and get the experience. Participate. Experiment. If you start feeling too comfortable, you're not challenging yourself!

YOUR ASSIGNMENT:
Overcoming Discomfort and
Procrastination

FRIPPICISM

Challenge everything you do.
Expand your thinking.
Refocus your efforts.
Rededicate yourself to your future.

Some things that make me uncomfortable are:

Which of these things will I push against to extend my comfort zone? How?

One thing I usually put off is:

To overcome this, I will:

My first step will be:

My time frame is:

CHAPTER 5

Self-Image and Confidence

FRIPPICISM
Artisans teach by what they do. *Masters teach by who they are.* *What artisans do is who they are.* *What masters do is who they are not.*
Robert Fripp

"One thing you should know about me is that I'm stupid," said Arthur L. Schawlow. The 1981 Nobel Prize winner was talking to an astonished class of undergraduates at the University of California, Berkeley. "But," he continued, "lots of people are stupid, which is kind of nice. It means they miss a lot of things. If you can discover one of the things they've missed, you may win a Nobel Prize too."

You can bet those students left the room with increased confidence in their own ability to make a difference in the world.

Seeing Yourself

"When people see themselves—really see themselves—they see what they are capable of becoming," insists Bert Decker of Decker Communications. People's inadequacies are much greater in their own minds than in anybody else's.

"For instance, when people hear themselves on audio tape, they say, 'Whose voice is that? It doesn't sound like me.'

People think they come across worse than they actually do. And the first time they see themselves on video, they're in shock. But after once, twice, three times, they begin looking at themselves objectively and they think, 'Hey, nobody can see my knees shaking, my butterflies fluttering. Nobody can see what I did behind the barn ten years ago or all the inadequacies I have because my mother told me to be all the things that I'm not.'

"A sixty-year-old woman came in," says Decker. "She worked for her son and he sent her. She was a rather meek housewife type, dominated by her husband. Her son ran a string of successful insurance companies. She managed one of his small offices in Los Angeles and did some selling on the telephone, but she didn't enjoy it because she was so shy.

"Her son, who had taken our video-feedback communications course, sent all his people through it. She came in, saw the lights and the cameras, and thought it was a seminar, a lecture where somebody else was about to speak. When she realized she would be speaking, she became terrified, but she had guts enough to get up there the first time and talk about herself. She was frightened, believe me, and after she saw herself, she was traumatized. She felt as if she looked thirty years older than her sixty years.

"But at the end of two days, she announced, 'We were supposed to hire someone to sell while I ran the office, but I'm going back to do the selling, and we'll hire somebody *else* to run the office.' This was a woman who had spoken in public only three times in her life, two of which were toasts at weddings, but she now saw herself as a competent and successful presenter."

Saying "Yes" to Yourself

Saying "yes" to yourself means acknowledging what you have that's good and working on what isn't. At one of my speaking engagements, I had the good fortune to meet Nina Fortin, a superb example of someone who said "yes."

When Nina was nine years old, in Italy during World War II, she was standing outside her grandmother's store. A twenty-four-year-old American soldier came over to her, took her by the hand, and asked to meet her parents. When he met them, they exchanged addresses and he said, "This is the cleanest little girl in town." Three years later, when Nina was twelve, her parents received a note from the American asking whether he could marry her when she grew up. When Nina was fifteen, her mother died and she had to help raise her younger brothers and sisters, the youngest of whom was only eleven months old.

Two years later, the American soldier returned to Italy to marry Nina. Her father told her she probably could not do any better, he was probably a rich American, and she should marry him and go to America. She did.

In America, though she could not speak one word of English, she went to work in a factory near Cleveland. For the first year of her marriage, Nina couldn't even talk to her husband. Later they moved to California, and she got a job cleaning model homes for a real estate company. One of the agents showing a house suggested, "Nina, why don't you get a real estate license and sell real estate?" She replied, "Well, not only can I not read English, but because Mussolini closed the schools during the war, I've had only two years of education in my own language."

Nina talked to her husband about the agent's suggestion. Her husband was unsupportive, but after many days of thinking, she told him, "If you will not buy some sort of insurance policy that absolutely guarantees I am totally looked after if you die, then I must be my own insurance policy."

So Nina went to school to get a real estate license. It wasn't easy for her. One day she asked the teacher, "What is that pimple?" He said, "What pimple?" It was a decimal point, and she did not know what it was or what it was called. But her teacher was very sympathetic and helped her.

After she got her license, she went on to get her broker's license, which requires a more complicated test. The first time she took the brokers' exam, she failed by one-and-a-half points. The second time, she passed. "I was taking this exam with really educated people, CPAs, lawyers," she explained. On her first try, she met a CPA who was taking the exam for the ninth time. He failed and didn't pass until his tenth try.

"How come you got it on your second try, but it took me ten times?" the CPA asked her later.

"I passed because I'm ignorant," Nina told him. "And because I'm ignorant, I listen to what the teacher says, and I do what he tells me. You failed because you're so smart. You have to argue every point. You may debate well, but I think you are more interested in showing off to the class than in learning."

Sometimes smart people outsmart themselves. Nina passed the exam because she knew something about life. It's an old story: When you don't have an education, you're forced to use your brain. Obstacles and limitations—even severe ones— can be overcome. *Life* magazine published a story about Nina Fortin's life, a story well worth remembering. Years later, I ran into Nina again at a convention in Las Vegas. She's still doing exceptionally well.

Above-Average Human Beings

As we strive to improve ourselves, we should emphasize our accomplishments rather than our failures. At a self-improvement seminar in San Francisco, the seminar leader asked the group of 350 how many of them thought they were above average. My hand shot up. Then he asked, "How many of you think you are below average?" A few people put their hands up.

One was a tiny woman in the back row. The leader ran back to her and began asking her questions. "You don't understand," she told him. "I can't read or write English very well."

This woman had come over from Italy twenty-nine years before. She had traveled widely in Europe and America, and she spoke three languages fluently. She had a good knowledge of American history because she had studied to become a citizen, and on her own she had raised three children, all successful in college. This woman had held the same job as a waitress for eleven years. She owned her own home, paid for free and clear, and had $5,000 in the bank. But she didn't consider herself above average because she couldn't read or write English well. The seminar leader began "grading" her on the different areas of her life. "Well," he said, "we have to give you 90 percent for personal finances, 100 percent for parenting...." and so on. For skill at reading and writing English, he gave her only twenty percent, but her cumulative score, on the leader's scale, was 72 percent, definitely above average.

The point is that comparing ourselves to others is usually pointless. When we design our own scale of values, all of us are well above "average" in what counts in our own lives.

Attitude or Education?

No matter how good we look or how sophisticated we are, too often we concentrate on the things we don't do well instead of patting ourselves on the back for all the good things we do. In the past, I have been intimidated by my own lack of education. Then I found out that, according to Stanford Research Institute, success is 88 percent attitude and 12 percent education. That made sense to me, and it was just the inspiration I needed. What is your inspiration?

A prosperous lawyer friend of mine is successful as a sharp negotiator and investor in real estate. I asked him, as I have asked many other successful people, whether he thought being successful stems from education or from innate intelligence. "It definitely comes from inner smarts," he replied. The kind of smarts he meant are not necessarily intelligence, although the successful people he knows would not make stupid decisions or take foolish risks. "They just act on things a lot faster than the average person," he added. "They can weigh things and make up their minds more quickly. They know they can do it, they believe they can, and they do." So inner drive and inner talent, and especially a belief in oneself, count much more than IQ as tools for success.

Comparing Yourself to Others

Probably the best thing that ever happened to me was growing up with a brilliant brother only one year younger than I. He was always at the top of his class, and I was always somewhere near the middle, so I got the impression I was not as smart as others. This made me work harder. Not that I ever experienced what is called sibling rivalry. My mother did a magnificent job of making each of us feel special.

What I got from my brother was not any sense of inferiority but a lifelong appreciation of the results that come from good work habits. As a child, I never missed school, for fear I would get behind. Although I didn't win anything else, I had perfect attendance certificates for years. One day in my middle twenties, I looked around to see whether I was still keeping up and discovered everyone else was miles behind!

How did this happen? I had developed good work habits. On Tuesday evenings, during my hairstyling apprenticeship, all the students would practice by doing models' hair. The other students would work on one or two models. I would always do five. Many evenings I also would practice on my neighbors' hair. Then, at the age of eighteen, I left home and went to live on an island off the coast of France. There I worked in a salon with some sophisticated gentlemen from the West End of London. They could do hairstyles I had never seen before, but they believed lunch hours were for eating lunch. I believed lunch hours were for squeezing three extra customers in. One day my boss told me I actually produced 30 percent more income for the salon than the stylists who were more talented, just by doing more.

When I arrived in San Francisco and worked at the Mark Hopkins Hotel, my boss had never seen anyone work like me. He said, "Patricia, will you go back to England and bring over twenty of your friends? I'll become a multi-millionaire!"

"I don't know twenty other people in England who work like me," I replied.

As the modern philosopher Woody Allen said, "Eighty percent of life is just turning up."

The Deciding Moment

Ten o'clock on a Tuesday morning, November 1972, I walked out in the lobby of the posh hairstyling salon where I worked, and there was Larry. He was a computer programmer for Levi Strauss, a real "nerd" before I even knew what one was or dreamed of becoming one. He was kind of pudgy and his hair was slicked down. Someone had told him, "You need Miss Fripp." He obviously wasn't sure about that, and he was distinctly uncomfortable in this unfamiliar setting.

I took him back to my booth, made a fuss over him, shampooed, fluffed, and styled his hair. When I was through, he looked *good.* He didn't know it yet, but he did. He walked out with his little bag of shampoo, conditioner, brush, and hairspray so he could keep looking good—I was as shameless a marketer then as I am now. When he got back to Levi Strauss, the women went wild. He went home, and his wife went wild. After this response, he started thinking that maybe he did look pretty good. He became a regular client.

Soon he was motivated to lose a little weight and engage in a little banter. He started acting in a more outgoing way. Levi Strauss noticed and offered him a sales position even though he had no prior sales experience. Larry turned out to be one of their most successful salespeople. In a very short time, his territory was split five times, his income almost tripled, and he began enjoying his work in a way he had never dreamed possible.

Am I saying this happened all because of a haircut? No. But his changed appearance changed his feelings about himself. He was inspired to act more confidently, and new opportunities opened up.

I was also inspired when I realized how I could influence people's lives in a positive way. I began jumping out of bed with even more enthusiasm each morning. Can I take full credit for transforming this man's life? Well, obviously Larry had something to do with it. I challenge you to find your own Larry. Find what you do in your job and in your world that makes the difference in other people's lives.

A $1000 Investment

Don't confuse spending money to impress others with making a good investment in your business and yourself. For instance, I insist on quality stationery and publicity materials, on maintaining a first-class office, and on presenting myself as a top professional. But I don't waste a penny on flashy cars or a second home I don't have time to visit.

Twenty years ago, communications expert Joan Minninger decided to expand the successful seminars she had been doing for the Civil Service Commission into training programs for major corporations. She made two investments totaling $1000—a lot of money at the time and a major sacrifice for Joan, who was existing month-to-month after a divorce. "I went to one of the best stores in town and spent $500 for one designer outfit with two silk blouses. That was my uniform. At the time, $500 was a lot of money for an outfit, but I decided I was going to hit the corporate world. The other big expenditure was $500 for watermarked stationery. I later learned my first big contract at General Electric was partly due to that stationery. The training manager liked my presentation, but the clincher was the fancy paper. In fact, my future husband later confessed the reason we met, the only reason he attended one of my seminars, was that the training manager was so enthusiastic about the paper. 'She must be dynamite. Look at that watermarked stationery!'"

Of course Joan had the talent to follow through. She has written a half-dozen successful books including *Total Recall*: *How to Boost Your Memory Power*, which has sold over 175,000 copies, and worked for a dozen major corporations—but it was the initial "package" that got her in the door.

FRIPPICISM

Never spend money just to impress people who don't care about you.
Never spend money just to impress people who do care about you.

What Your Hands Say

Even small details of personal grooming can affect how other people perceive you. One of my customers from my salon days, Al Stanton, told me about a friend named Lyle Guslander. The two went to Alameda High School together. After they graduated, Lyle Guslander went to Cornell University and studied hotel administration. After college, he became the assistant manager of a large hotel in San Francisco.

One day, walking along Market Street in San Francisco, Al Stanton met Lyle, who invited him to look around the hotel. Lyle was animated and talked a lot with his hands. After Al had been escorted all over, he said to Lyle, "Do you mind if I give you some friendly criticism? Your fingernails are absolutely terrible. They are broken, uneven, and dirty. You speak so much with your hands—you're almost constantly showing brochures and price lists to people—it really gives a bad first impression." Lyle never forgot that advice.

Soon after this, Lyle went to Hawaii and acquired many hotels including the Royal Lahaina Resort. Several years later, Al Stanton was in Hawaii and went to see his old friend. Lyle welcomed Al and then called his staff into the office. "This is the gentleman who made me aware of how much appearance and grooming can improve your chance for success," he told them.

"He made me aware I had to change my poorly manicured hands."

Now, maybe Lyle Guslander would have become very successful anyway. But by *not* turning people off along the way with dirty fingernails, he obviously did his career a favor.

When Opportunity Knocks, Be Dressed for It

I've already told you how I first met Diane Parente when she came to one of my presentations. I'll tell that story again here to make a new point. The presentation I was delivering was in a major department store. I was wandering through the audience, as I usually do, introducing myself to the people in attendance. Out of the corner of my eye, I noticed one of the most stunning women I'd ever seen. She was the only one there who was wearing a hat. She'd never been to one of the store's presentations before, but when she read about it, something told her to come. Fate destined us to meet—and to dress up.

When I learned Diane was a wardrobe consultant with fourteen years in the fashion industry, I told her she should be giving workshops and introduced her to the store manager. He booked her to speak at one of their programs a month or so later.

She said 'yes' immediately, even though she had never given talks before. (If she had thought about it, she might well have said 'no,' blocking a whole new area for her career.) Since that day, I have used her services and have recommended her to dozens of other people. We've also become best friends. This is a perfect example of how looking successful helps you sell your services.

The Odds for Failure

If you expect failure, the odds are overwhelming you will fail. Having confidence you will succeed improves the probability of success. To achieve success, then, a person must develop self-confidence, learn not to fear risk. The only way to do that is actually to try something that results in the feeling of success.

Many of us are unsuccessful and unadventurous because we tried something once, didn't do it well, and have never tried again. I can remember several years ago when I started demonstrating haircutting. The audiences were so unimpressed, I pitied myself. But by getting up time and time again, I slowly became one of the top hairstyling demonstrators in the country. Whenever I stood up to try again, I concentrated on how good I was going to be in the future instead of reliving the unsuccessful past attempts. Time and practice improve us.

A Cure for Swollen Egos

The most positive self-image can benefit from an occasional reality check. Once I gave an especially good speech, a customer service seminar for the community of Rehoboth Beach, Delaware. My triumph was written up in the local newspaper. It was written up on page 16, in the sports section, right next to the obituaries, just above the fire and police announcements. And just to be sure I didn't get a swelled head, they spelled my name "Flipp." It's okay to get taken down a peg if you still accept that who you are is okay with you and what you are doing is for yourself.

Who Would You Rather Be?

Being a better person...isn't that what it's all about? When we are disenchanted, we should question ourselves and realize we are capable of changing things more than we give ourselves credit for. Ask yourself:
- Is there anyone else on earth I would like to be?
- Is there any other place I would like to be?
- Is there any other career I would rather pursue?

Hopefully, you will also realize some of the great things you've already gotten and achieved.

Too Late for Self-Esteem?

Self-esteem, of course, starts quite early. Many people at seminars tell me it's too late for them—utter nonsense, of course—but they wish their kids could hear what I have to say. Even if you have bought the fable that it's too late for you, it is important to start influencing your children positively.

My friend Jeanne Robertson, President of the National Speakers Association the year after me and one of the top humorous speakers in the country, says that, when she was thirteen, she was six feet two inches tall with size eleven feet. She is sure her parents used to close their door at night and say, "Oh, my God, she's still growing." But her parents never let her think anything was wrong, Jeanne says. "You think children are cruel, but when I was thirteen, walking down the street trying to get my arms and legs going in the same direction, grown men would come up and look at me and say, 'Hey, little girl, how tall are you?'"

When she went to visit relatives, they would invariably say, "My, how you've grown!" Jeanne's parents helped her with comic retorts. With their coaching, she would beat her relatives to it, jumping out of the car and shouting, "Oh my, how I've grown!" Her parents developed not only her sense of humor but her self-esteem, two things all of us can use in abundance. Jeanne is famous for showing people how to accept and laugh at the things they can't change.

Mother Knew Best

My mother told me, "It is the inside of you that's important. That's why you need to dress up and look good—so you attract people who can then find out how nice, interesting, and valuable you are."

YOUR ASSIGNMENT:
What Am I Telling Others?

FRIPPICISM

*Style is being yourself,
but on purpose.*

1. Do I dress neatly and appropriately for each business occasion? YES NO

2. Is my eye communication good and steady? YES NO

3. Is my posture comfortable and self-confident? YES NO

4. Do I sit erect? YES NO

5. Are my gestures natural? YES NO

6. Do I give the appearance of being self-confident, even when I'm not? YES NO

7. Is my voice natural and my conversation spontaneous?
   YES NO

8. Do I have any mannerisms that others might find annoying?
   YES NO

9. Do I use non-words like "ur," "uh," and "ah"? YES NO

10. Am I a good listener?   YES   NO

11. Have I ever listened to a recording of myself in an important situation? (If not, why not?)   YES   NO

12. If I met somebody important in the supermarket early on Saturday morning, would I feel I had to apologize for my appearance?   YES   NO

13. Do I take sincere interest in other people when I first meet them? (Or am I too concerned about what they may be thinking of me?)   YES   NO

Homework Assignment

If the answer to any of the above questions is "No," what are you going to do about it? Decide on one specific action you will take. Write your action plan here.

CHAPTER 6

Marketing Yourself

FRIPPICISM

There is no point going anywhere that people won't remember you were there.

A woman at a Credit Union National Association convention asked me where I got my degree in behavioral psychology. "Behind a hairstyling chair," I told her, "a twenty-four year degree." Yes, I started young. I've observed that many successful businesspeople began their entrepreneurship at an early age. One of my hairstyling clients, a multi-millionaire in his forties, told me his first successful scheme, at age eight, was selling lizards and snakes. He had a great money-making venture until the city of Palo Alto closed him down. Today he runs a number of more conventional businesses.

Jim Longman, a successful life insurance salesman I met at a Dale Carnegie class, also discovered his selling ability at age eight. One winter in Shenandoah, Iowa, he arrived a bit late for his Cub Scout meeting. The leader of the den was explaining that the Scouts had to sell one hundred boxes of Christmas cards. The money would go to the church charity. Not realizing that the hundred boxes was the goal for the whole troop of Scouts, the boy trudged through the snow, knocking on doors every day after school, showing samples of cards, and collecting money. At the next Scout meeting, he was heartbroken to report he had sold only ninety-eight boxes of cards. The leader stood in total disbelief—until the boy emptied the money from his pockets onto the table.

> FRIPPICISM
>
> *It's amazing how often we manage to live up to what we think is demanded.*

While in college, Longman had a terrific idea. He contacted the parents of his fellow students and asked if they'd like to have personalized birthday cakes and other goodies delivered to their beloved offspring who were far from home. In a short period of time, he had such a good business that he hired other students to do all the legwork. As a young man, he developed the habit of thinking creatively. No wonder he is a success today. (Lizards, snakes, and cakes aside, what was the great idea you had but never did anything about?)

Creating the Entrepreneurial Ethic

When I was five, my younger brother and I participated in a ritual every Saturday night. We would stand before our parents in the kitchen, and they would ask, "What did you do this week to earn your pocket money?" For every good thing we had done, we earned a penny. I couldn't have pronounced the word at the time, but this experience encouraged me to think entrepreneurially. I thank my father for that early lesson which I remember as "the harder you work and the more good things you do, the more you are rewarded."

As children, my brother and I frequently sold our used comic books by the front gate to earn extra money. Years later I heard about Mike, the twelve-year-old son of one of my hairstyling clients, Ernie Choenis, a true entrepreneur. Mike learned a friend had made $17 one weekend by painting house numbers on neighbors' curbs. The friend was content with his weekend's profits, but Mike decided to expand the idea into a real business. He borrowed initial startup capital from his parents, purchased stencils, paint, and brushes, and practiced painting numbers. Then he contacted hundreds of people. To save time, he called prospects on the telephone at night. After quickly repaying the loan to his parents, he made a healthy profit.

This lad, a true entrepreneur, then subcontracted the work to his brother, who received a dollar less for performing the service. I told Ernie Choenis how much his son impressed me with his fabulous moneymaking ideas. Ernie replied that, although his children had a comfortable life because of his success, he did not lavish pocket money on them. They were encouraged to be imaginative and make the most of themselves. I have always maintained that one of the best things we can do for children is to teach them the value of money. Recently at a Bank of America awards program, a self-made millionaire disagreed. He said, "It's not one of the best things parents can do. It's *the* best thing!"

The Kid and the Chocolates

Steve Hudson, a manager with American Express in Phoenix, Arizona, told me how he'd visited a large, upscale mall to get ten gift boxes of chocolates for employees who'd just finished a big project. There were two candy stores, exactly opposite each other. He popped his head in the door of the first one and said, "Excuse me, do you accept American Express?"

"Yes," said the clerk. So Hudson picked out about $150 worth of candy and took it to the counter. On the cash register were two signs: "MasterCard" and "Visa." No American Express symbol. Hudson looked across at the candy store opposite, and on the door he could see the distinctive green American Express logo.

"You know," he said to the cashier. "I work for American Express. I know you accept our card, but you don't advertise us and that store opposite does. I really have to take my business over there." The clerk nodded that she understood.

If you had been that clerk, what would you have done? What would the people looking after your business do? Fortunately there was another clerk in this store, a bright young man of sixteen who was stocking the shelves and wiping the counter. The sixteen-year-old wasn't prepared to let a customer walk out without fighting for the business. He knew a $150 purchase in a candy store would probably be the biggest individual sale of the day. He also knew that, once you sell someone, they develop the habit of coming back over and over. The value of a happy customer is worth the extra effort to retain the business. (Bill Gates said, "Whenever you lose a customer, you lose two ways. One, you don't get their money. Two, your competitors do.")

Before Hudson could turn and leave the store, this sixteen-year-old cried out, "Sir, hold on just a moment." He ran across the walkway to the other candy store and grabbed an American Express credit application. Then he raced back, cut out the logo, and taped it to the register above the other credit card logos. "Sir," he said, "is that good enough?"

This young man was working after school for minimum wage, but he took the initiative. He creatively removed the obstacle to doing business with this customer. He certainly never said to himself, "They're not paying me enough to think." He made a mundane job exciting by rising to a challenge and solving a problem.

And since he is a teenager, this go-getting young man probably spends several hours a night surfing the World Wide Web. If you're not yet a techie, maybe this will inspire you. Imagine what will happen when this young man comes into your territory in a few years. What awesome competition!

Ideas from Bright Young Executives

Another of my former hairstyling clients, John Wright, is the owner of a successful financial investment company in San Francisco. He went to work right out of college for a major airline. Soon he was a young executive, up-and-coming, bright, and with good ideas. One day he figured out how to save the airline a lot of money. At the time, the executives who had the biggest budgets were paid more and had more power. John convinced the company that instead of rewarding people for spending more money and controlling bigger budgets, it should reward people for *saving* money. His idea was just common sense, but it made that company a million dollars. When the company rewarded him with a measly $200-a-month raise, he realized he could do better on his own. Although he had planned a career with the airline, he chucked it and moved to California. "I figured if I'm going to do what I'm doing, I can do it anywhere, and I'd rather live in California."

The lesson we can learn from John Wright is not about how bright this young man was—his brainstorm evolved from common sense—or how much money he actually saved a huge corporation, but his habit of thinking creatively. The point is, you can start anywhere from scratch, but the "scratch" begins with the process of thinking about where you are and where you want to be.

Sitting in the Right Chair

My friend Anne Ratcliffe had a new job with a technology company. Her first project was getting people to attend a big conference. She was talking to a potential attendee on the phone when she realized he was also a customer of her company. "Immediately I switched to a sales and marketing mode," says Anne. "I interviewed him, found out what he thought about the company, and made some suggestions about how he could use our products better. When I hung up, I realized the vice president of sales was standing behind me. 'Who were you talking to,' he asked, 'and why did you say what you did?'" Anne was so new, she feared she'd done something wrong.

The vice president continued, "That was the most brilliant presentation I've ever heard. How did you know to do all that?" I asked Anne how he had happened to overhear. She replied, "I was sitting in the *right chair!*" There was a work station just outside his office. The more experienced people had all refused to take it, fearing their lapses might be overheard. Anne, being the new kid on the block, got the spot no one else wanted.

How can you position yourself so the people who can do you some good know how good you are without your seeming too pushy? Sitting in the *right chair* helps.

Report the Deals, Not the Details

When you are reporting to a higher-up, describe the deals, not the details. I had a friend who managed a small professional group. They were always hard up, and she had to justify her existence. I said, "Let me look at the report you sent to the Board. One of the items was, "sent 20 faxes." I said, "No you didn't. That's the details. Report on the deals. You personally invited twenty Ford dealers to hear your speaker from Ford. Fourteen attended at a profit of $17 each. Two of them joined, at a $450 profit to the organization. That's the bottom line. So you didn't just send twenty faxes."

It's all in how you present your ideas and your value. If you have brilliant ideas but insufficient confidence to share them, you will get no credit for having them. Sharing is part of selling yourself.

My job is teaching people how to develop professional business relationships. What I do for fun is teach people to use the same skills in social situations. If you're a single person in a social group and you don't have the confidence to walk over and introduce yourself to an interesting-looking person of the opposite sex, you probably lack the self-confidence in a business meeting to walk over and introduce yourself to the manager, no matter how good it might be for your career. It's the same skill. Speaking one-on-one is just as important as learning to speak to a thousand people.

Everyone Can Be Creative

There are dozens of small ways you can regenerate yourself and those around you when you add a personal, creative signature to your work. Barbara Glanz, who wrote *Care Packages for the Workplace*, told me about a supermarket bagger named Johnny who has Down syndrome. A few weeks after she'd spoken to a large group of supermarket employees, Johnny called her. He said he'd liked her presentation so much, that he'd gone home that night and asked his father to show him how to use the computer. Each night when he goes home, he looks through books and magazines for a *Thought for the Day*. When he can't find one he likes, he makes up one himself. Then he types it over and over on the page and prints it out, cutting the pages into small strips like the ones in fortune cookies, and signing each *Thought* on the back.

The next day, as he bags people's groceries, he adds his *Thought for the Day* in each bag with a flourish, adding his own personal touch in a heartwarming, fun, and creative way.

A month later, the manager of Johnny's store phoned Barbara Glanz and said, "You won't believe what happened today. When I went out on the floor this morning, the line at Johnny's checkout stand was three times longer than any other line. I went ballistic. 'Get more lanes open,' I said. But the customers said, 'No, we want to be in Johnny's lane. We want our *Thought for the Day*.'" One woman even told him she now shopped every time she passed the store rather than once a week because she wanted her *Thought for the Day*. Imagine what this does to the bottom line. The manager ended his conversation with Barbara by asking, "Who do you think is the most important person in our store?" Johnny, of course.

Three months later, the manager called Barbara again. He said, "Johnny has transformed our store. Now, in our floral department, when they have a broken flower or an unsold corsage, they go out on the floor and find an older woman or a little girl and pin it on them. One of our meat packers loves Snoopy, so he bought 50,000 Snoopy stickers and every time he prepares a package of meat, he puts a sticker on it. We are having so much fun. That is spirit in the workplace."

> **FRIPPICISM**
>
> *If you always act as if your name is on the door, it soon will be.*

I urge you to write an overall marketing strategy for your career and your life. When you market anything, including yourself, your efforts have to be ongoing, consistent, relentless, high-tech, low-tech, no-tech, and (in my case) totally shameless. The magic is in the mix.

YOUR ASSIGNMENT:
Ideas for Selling Yourself

> FRIPPICISM
>
> *If you have great ideas and no confidence to share them, you will not get credit for having them.*

Some great ideas I've never followed up on are:

The one I select to follow up on now is:

The first thing I'll do is:

My time frame will be:

Homework Assignment

Start a Great Idea diary. Write them down and decide the best way to pursue them. Regularly record your progress and the outcome of your strategies. Then pat yourself on the back for your follow-through, and share your successes with a friend.

CHAPTER 7

Boosting Your Business Image

> ### FRIPPICISM
>
> *It is not your customer's job to remember you. It's your obligation and responsibility to make sure you are not forgotten.*

Suppose someone wants to do business with you. What is his or her first impression? What do they see, hear, smell, feel? When we try to influence people to think favorably of us, we engage in what executive Marie Randall calls "impression management." It is essential to good business that we do this consciously and conscientiously all the time.

The Crucial Four Minutes

The first four minutes of any business encounter can make or break your future relationship with a prospective client. In *Contact: The First Four Minutes*, author Leonard Zunin says, "Why four minutes? It is not an arbitrary interval. Rather, it is the average time, demonstrated by careful observation, during which strangers in a social situation interact before they decide to part or continue their encounter."

The way the client is greeted, the way the waiting room looks, even the colors, light level, and odors of the room contribute significantly to how customers will like the service they get. The best product is unlikely to survive a negative first impression. (More about "five-sensing" later in this chapter.) My father once said we should ask ourselves, "Would I want to do business with somebody who looks, acts, and talks like me?"

Every Employee is a P.R. Specialist

Every member of a group represents that group. Everyone connected with a business, even the floor sweeper and the receptionist's boyfriend who hangs around the front desk waiting to take her for lunch, is an active member of that firm's Public Relations Department.

As both a hairstylist and, now, a professional speaker, I am constantly trying to make my clients' experience with me pleasant. I learned the value of this at age fifteen from my first boss, Mr. Paul. He treated every woman, while she was in our salon, as though she were the only person in the world. And he saw to it that everyone in his organization treated his customers with the same respect.

Later, in San Francisco, I heard a story with a similar moral from one of my customers, Al Stanton. He had worked in the traffic department of the Zellerbach Paper Company early in his career. Isadore Zellerbach, the founder of the company, was a very personable man who believed in making all his employees feel important. Zellerbach frequently asked Al's advice on different matters. Al was puzzled that such an important man would be concerned with the opinions of even the lowest employees, but Zellerbach explained why all his employees needed to feel they were part of the company.

Early in the history of the company, a Zellerbach truck was following a rather fancy car on a narrow road. The truck driver was impatient to pass and kept honking. After about fifteen minutes, when he finally did pass, he put his head out the window and said, "You #&!*, you want to take up the whole road?" Then he roared off, the Zellerbach name all over the truck.

The gentleman driving the car was the owner of the company that was Zellerbach's best customer in the area. When he returned to his office, furious, he ordered the purchasing department to cancel all orders with Zellerbach and never buy anything from the company again.

It was several months before this lost account came to the attention of Mr. Zellerbach. Trying to get the former client on the phone proved fruitless, so Zellerbach went to the company to talk to this man in person. When he heard about the Zellerbach truck incident, he was shocked—shocked he had overlooked one of the most important factors in his business: absolutely every employee represents the company. From that time on, Zellerbach's truck drivers received lessons in politeness and human relations.

FRIPPICISM

Technology does not run an enterprise, relationships do.

I had quite a different experience with a restaurant. My friends and I used to meet regularly for breakfast at the Pepper Mill Restaurant in Serramonte, near San Francisco. We'd race in at 7:00 a.m. and be greeted by a waitress named Judy, always a pleasure to see bright and early in the morning. One Christmas, I was pleasantly surprised to see she had brought little Christmas presents for her regular customers.

One man's experience with a truck driver influenced his relationship to an entire company. Our experiences with a waitress influenced our relationship with an entire restaurant chain. That's why there is nothing more important to an organization than hiring the best people to represent the company and then helping all of them to recognize their role as public relations specialists.

The Most Expensive Worker

One worker's poor performance can cost a company incalculable losses in both dollars and goodwill. I found that out when I went to buy my first car at the age of twenty-nine. Knowing absolutely nothing about cars, I asked the advice of a few clients and friends, who convinced me I should get one of three makes. One Wednesday afternoon, determined to buy a car, I walked into the first dealership, met a friendly young salesman, and announced, "I wish to buy a car. I want a hatchback, and I want to pay cash. How much is this one?" He told me and took me out for a drive. We laughed, joked, and had a good time. He said, "I understand you're shopping around. This is how much it will be. If you're interested, come back and see me."

Strolling down the street, I came to the second dealer. I said, "Good afternoon. I would like to buy a car. I want to pay cash and I want a hatchback. How much?" They informed me they did not have a hatchback. I thanked them, and continued on to the third dealership.

I should have guessed what was about to happen as the salesman walked toward me. His hair was totally disheveled and a cigar butt was hanging out of his mouth. In the friendliest possible way, I said, "Good afternoon. I would like to buy a car. I want to pay cash and I want a hatchback. How much is this one?" I turned to a glistening model on my left. His reply was gruff, "Look at the sticker price, lady." No sticker was in sight. Here I was, prepared to write a check for whatever the car cost (if it had been the one I wanted), and the salesman couldn't even be polite.

I enjoy spending money. I enjoy listening to a good sales presentation. And I like people to appreciate my business. But I will not pay money to someone who is not civil and does not make the transaction enjoyable. Turning on my heels, without looking at the sticker price, I walked out of the showroom and bought a car from the helpful salesman back at dealership number one. Certainly, the car offered by that third dealer is an excellent car. The company probably spends many millions of dollars each year on advertising. But I will never buy one.

Nearly every professional woman over forty has a similar horror story. When my friend Sheila Murray Bethel first achieved financial success, she set out one morning to buy the car of her dreams. She walked into the dealership, looked at the various models, sat in them, opened and closed doors. She was ready to write a check on the spot. But no salesperson acknowledged her presence. Maybe they thought she couldn't afford their cars.

When she finally located a salesman, he said, "If you see something you like, let me know," and walked away. She pursued him and started to ask questions about models. The salesman stopped her: "Why don't you bring your husband in and we can talk seriously." Needless to say, she stormed out, walked down the street, and bought a car from a different dealership. And she has continued to buy that brand of car ever since. Happily, this dismissive attitude toward women car buyers has begun to change.

But even male customers can run into astonishing ineptitude by salespeople who are supposed to be representing their companies. My friend Chris Hegarty stopped early one morning at a car dealer on "automobile row" in San Francisco, sincerely interested in buying. All the salesmen were huddled in a corner. One came over to Chris and said, "I'm sorry. I can't help you. We're having a sales meeting."

Your Weakest Link

I was on a program with noted broadcaster Paul Harvey who said, "For a company's advertising strategy to work, it has to be handled not only corporately but also individually." Years ago, when "Big" Randy Tobias was the boss of AT&T Communications before he went to Eli Lilly, he came up with a very simple rule: "Whoever picks up the phone owns the problem."

You've probably had the same experience I have. I called one company thirteen times, and thirteen times I heard, "He's not at his desk. He's not at his desk. He's not at his desk." Finally I said, "Then, drag the desk to where he is!" If you want to improve your customer service, don't do what irritates you when you're a customer.

Companies, both large and small, spend a fortune promoting their image to the public. Yet it takes only one person to ruin that image. Management's biggest concern today is to make all employees, including the filing clerk, the janitor, and the stock clerk, realize the important part they play in the company's plans. A manager's biggest problem is to help the lesser-paid employees understand their roles in the bigger picture, and to boost their self-image by demonstrating how much they contribute to the company's success.

Real People, Extraordinary Jobs

What about the so-called "real people"? The ones who answer the phones and type the letters? The people who meet the public face to face? They are the biggest public relations department in any company, yet some managers think, "Well, we don't pay them much. They're not going to be around long enough to worry about their contribution to our image."

A major chain of jewelers I worked with wanted to monitor customer service. They sent shoppers into their stores to report on their experiences. Without exception, the problems were always with the newest or part-time employees. And what did the managers say? "Well, you can't expect the part-time person to be as good as the full-time person."

"Why not?" I asked. "If they're not, they're going to lose customers for you!" As my friend and fellow speaker Jim Cathcart puts it, "Sales is an attitude, not a department."

A furniture representative told me of a friend of his who owned a furniture store. A nice young salesman used to call on him regularly once a month. Because the store was in a hard-to-reach, outlying area of Oklahoma, and because the salesman was always cheerful and always took time to call on him, the owner felt bad he couldn't give the salesman any business.

One day the owner decided that the next time the young man came in, he would place an order. The salesman arrived. The owner said, "I want to talk to you. Can you wait? A customer has just come in." He dealt with the customer for half an hour, and then returned to the young salesman. By this time the owner had decided *not* to buy anything from the salesman. Why? Because during that fateful half hour, the young man had sat reading a newspaper. He hadn't bothered to walk around the store to find out what it had in stock. His lack of initiative and real interest cost him the sale.

"Real people" are those in the front lines, the people who represent a company to the public every day but never get to fly in the corporate jet. One of my clients, Horst Schulze, is President and Chief Operating Officer for the Ritz-Carlton Hotels. "Whenever we open a new property," he told me, "I'm involved in the hiring and training." He puts all potential employees through a rigorous screening process. At the first training session, he tells the group, "We are all ladies and gentlemen serving ladies and gentlemen. It is your job to give our guests an *experience* because no one pays our prices just for a place to sleep. You will never tell a guest, 'It's not my job.' You will never bring your personal problems to work. I know some of you may not wish to work in an environment that expects so much from you, so we'll take a break now, and if you want to leave, you can do so without any embarrassment." I was surprised to learn that at each such session, a number of people don't return to their seats after the break.

"Surely, most people who want to work in the hospitality industry would want to work at the Ritz-Carlton!" I told him.

"No," he replied, "...because we expect so much."

Soon after, I was at the San Francisco Ritz-Carlton, speaking for the Missouri Bankers. As usual, I went early to schmooze with the audience members, and I stopped to chat with a waiter. "How long have you worked here?" I asked.

"Ever since we opened the property," he said. (I loved the "we" in his statement!)

"Is it true," I asked, "that they tell you a lot is expected of you, and then give you a chance to leave?"

"Oh, yes," he said. "But at the same time the Ritz-Carlton was opening, the Sheraton Palace Hotel had just invested millions in renovations and was also rehiring. Both are luxury hotels, so everyone who applied at one also applied at the other. But," he added, "the difference was night and day.

"At the Sheraton Palace, which is a spectacular hotel, it was like any other hotel opening. It was a cattle call. But, here at the Ritz-Carlton, there were comfortable places to sit. Free coffee and croissants were offered while we waited."

Do you understand what management was doing? They were modeling the behavior they expected from them before offering them a job. They didn't treat applicants like cattle. Instead, they told them, "You are ladies and gentlemen serving ladies and gentlemen." And, if for one moment you are thinking, 'but that's the Ritz-Carlton,' let me tell you that I've also worked for budget motel chains that live by exactly the same philosophy and do exactly the same things because they know people who can afford only $20.00 a night still know class.

This waiter recognized that you can't tell people they are ladies and gentlemen and then deal with them as if they were menials. The Ritz-Carlton was treating potential employees the same way they wanted those employees to treat the guests. It's not what you *say* you believe as an individual or company. It's what you model, encourage, reward, and let happen.

Your Image When No One Is Looking

Some people (and businesses) think a self-image is what other people see, while behind the scenes anything goes. But a true self-image reflects your true self, even when no one is looking.

The president of a company that sells gourmet coffees to hotels told me that one hot day he had been on his delivery truck at the Ritz-Carlton Hotel loading dock, looking quite ordinary in shirt sleeves and jeans. He asked a Ritz-Carlton employee if there was a drinking fountain. "Oh, don't worry," said the employee, "I'll bring you some water." A few moments later the man returned with a blue Ritz-Carlton glass filled with ice water and presented with a napkin, just as if he were an honored guest, not a workman on a truck. Obviously, the Ritz-Carlton has a powerful organizational self-image.

The Self-Satisfaction of Serving

There's a big difference between serving and being subservient. After working the ticket counter at U.S. Air (now U.S. Airways) for a number of years, Eileen O'Connell, one of my old running buddies, became a flight attendant. She told me many flight attendants don't want to work in first class because they think the customers will be more demanding.

"I thought it would be easier in first class," I said, "because there are fewer people to look after."

"Definitely," she replied, "but most people don't like to feel they have to serve the public. So many flight attendants have the attitude, 'it's us versus the passengers.' Me, I truly enjoy it. Someone the other day thanked me for being so nice. She said she'd never flown first class before, and I'd made it such a wonderful experience." Obviously, Eileen doesn't equate serving with being subservient. When I served my customers as a hair stylist, I never once felt servile or subservient. It was such a joy to treat people well, and they were so appreciative in return.

Eileen is the sort of employee who has always given her employer money-saving suggestions. Many of her ideas were rejected when she originally offered them, but they were later embraced when the airlines had to institute cost-saving measures. Eileen is one of those who do their job beyond their paycheck, just for the joy and self-satisfaction of making a contribution.

Your Worst Employee

"Your business is only as good as your worst employee." The first time I heard that, it affected my whole philosophy of business. In a small business, everybody counts. In a big company, you used to be able to hide incompetent people or ship them off to Podunk, but even then, they still had a negative impact.

My brother has founded several rock groups, in addition to playing in top rock bands. He insists you can ensure being able to handle problems when they arise "if your staff are fairly paid and well-treated. If you show them your confidence in their ability to solve problems, then they'll react positively when a problem comes up. But if you shout at your staff, if you underpay and belittle them, if you let them know they'll be sacked if they make a mistake, they'll leave you as soon as trouble starts...if not sooner."

Finding Mr. & Ms. Right

Good employees turn up in a company, not by magic, but through good hiring practices. I started hiring better people when I figured out what I was actually looking for. To do this, I began by making two lists. The first was a list of what I had to have from the people I hired. The second list covered what it would be nice to have.

Once I hired a woman because she had been recommended to me by someone who had supervised her as a waitress in a top hotel. My new employee had been to beauty school. I assumed that if she was a good cocktail waitress, she would be a good hairstylist, since both must know how to deal with the public. I didn't ask her some of the questions I now know to ask. Later I found out that, as a student, she had asked other people to clock her in and out of beauty school so she could accumulate enough hours for certification. Her attitude was, "What can they teach me?" This attitude didn't change when she came to work for me. I still had a lot to learn about hiring. No employee will ever be perfect, but there are faults you can work with and faults you can't.

Questions for Prospective Employees

The following questions can help you learn about the faults and strengths of people you are considering for a job. If you are on the other end of the interview, they can alert you to the effect of your answers to such questions.

Tell me about yourself. All the exciting and interesting things. People offer revealing replies to this question. So many people, even top executives, say, "Oh, there's nothing exciting about me." You find out about people's self-esteem when they answer this question.

If you could wave a magic wand and create a perfect environment to work in, what would it be like? Suppose the potential employee answers, "I don't like to have someone breathing down my neck. I like to be left on my own, to make up my mind how to do things." You know immediately that this is the wrong person for a job that's heavily supervised. If someone says, "I'm good at following directions," this person may perform poorly at a job where initiative is necessary or where he or she must work alone. If the applicant says, "Well, I like to work by myself in my own space," and the employee must share a crowded workspace with others whose personalities may conflict, you know you are likely to have an unhappy employee. Even when a quiet, personable individual replies, "I like to work with people, but I would rather have my own space," my experience shows that the work area quickly becomes a private domain. Would you put someone like that to work in a small space where people are constantly walking through to get to the coffee machine? If you do, the employee probably won't last in the job—or won't do the job well. Look at your options. If it is impossible to alter the workspace to accommodate the individual's preferences, keep looking.

Describe the best boss you ever had. What made him or her so special? Describe the worst boss. If the description of the worst boss sounds anything like you, you know that person won't be happy working with you.

What's your hobby? There are questions the law does not allow an employer to ask, whether a person is married for instance. But when I was hiring for my hairstyling salon, I needed to know something about a person's private life because I had to know if he or she could be at work by eight o'clock sharp. I asked people what they do when they are not working. I asked about their hobbies. I knew if someone liked to go out disco dancing five nights a week, he or she might not show up bright and early.

There's another list to make when you're hiring: what you can offer the prospective employee besides money. Enthusiasm, motivation, and persistence are rarely proportional to salary. Often they are in inverse ratio. (Why else would anyone choose to be an artist, performer, teacher, or writer?) What opportunities for growth, education, excitement, and achievement are you offering along with a paycheck? Self-motivated employees are great, but it never hurts to spotlight some incentives.

A Pie in the Kisser

How do you keep people highly motivated, productive, and eager to come to work in the morning, especially when many of them make barely more than the minimum wage? "Make the job fun," says George McKittrick, "and show them they can really make a difference by soliciting their feedback and acting on it." McKittrick has worked for many years with a big catalogue company, Foster & Gallagher, that offers food and horticulture items. Many of their large staff handle phone orders, making them the first contact a potential customer has with the company.

"The key," says McKittrick, "is never to allow anything to get stale, especially the environment." Some strategies were to hold a potluck every month, drinks provided by the company, and have work days built around a theme like St. Patrick's Day. Every summer, there was a week-long carnival where, for 50¢, anyone could purchase a paper plate loaded with frosting cream and hurl it at a manager. "You could see the eyes of the new employees widen—'Can I really do this to a vice president?'

"We stressed that this is a family business, so everyone is an owner, that they have the ear of the customers and are all advocates for them. Employees know that their feedback will affect what products will be offered in the future and, ultimately, the success of the company." This wasn't just an idle employee relations ploy. Information was gathered weekly, formalized in a newsletter *The Voice of the Customer* and sent to the team leaders. Bonuses of $500 were paid out, and more than a hundred changes made as a result of employee feedback. "It keeps everyone fresh and focused on the customer's needs, so shopping is an enjoyable experience for the customer as well."

Another executive who knows how to keep people motivated is Joe Peyton, the recently-retired General Manager of one of my clients, Fleetwood Homes. You may be surprised to learn that I've become an expert in the "manufactured housing world." Fleetwood builds the best, most spectacular homes and offers terrific customer service. I've been in their factories and called on their dealers. I've even called on their competitors, pretending to be a customer.

When I visited their Sacramento area plant, I asked Joe about how they kept their standards so high. "I can understand," I said, "how you keep people motivated when they have nice clean jobs, but what do you do when they've got a hard, dirty job on the assembly line? How do you get the message of quality and service and 'doing it right the first time' across to them?"

Joe said, "I just ask them, 'Are our customers as good as your mother? Would you want your mother to spend her hard-earned money on what you just made?'" Make customer service and quality and doing it right a *personal* thing. Leadership has to come from the bottom up. When you respect the intelligence of your employees, acknowledging their ability to improve your business, you do yourself two favors. Your business functions better, and your personnel turnover is lower.

Firing Your Mistakes

Someone in one of my workshops said, "It isn't a mistake until it gets out of the shop." Within every company there's a lot of room for legitimate experimentation. But there's a big difference between constructive risk-taking and outright incompetence.

After the former cocktail waitress had worked for me for several weeks, I realized I had made a mistake. I hadn't interviewed her properly. She wasn't what I expected. One day I said to her, "I made a mistake. I'm very sorry. I apologize to you. I shouldn't have hired you, but I'm not prepared to live with my mistake any longer. You're fired." She cried and said, "No one has ever fired me." I said, "It's my responsibility. I'm really sorry. I shouldn't have hired you." This experience taught me something important: I don't have to live with my mistakes.

Whether hiring or being hired, we need to realize how we —or the potential employee—will fit the organization and how well the organization fits us. When I was in Norfolk, Virginia, speaking to the Sales and Marketing Executives Club there, a gentleman came up to me afterward and said, "I lost a $10,000 order because a client came into our facility and spoke to the shipping clerk while I was down the street. The shipping clerk accused the client of stealing his pen!" Now, no employer should allow his employees to be harassed or intimidated in the name of good customer relations, but this was a faulty value call on the part of the clerk. Everyone has walked off with someone else's pen occasionally. All you have to do is politely ask for it back or chalk the thirty-nine cents up to public relations costs.

Good managers understand how important the people under them are. Joe Heitz's philosophy, which extends well beyond the working world, is "Be a part of the whole rather than the whole yourself." He meant that the Heitz Cellars winery was *all* the employees, not just Joe Heitz.

The Waitress Executive

The quality of work in every company would improve if all employees realized their own importance to the overall public relations picture. Once, in Nashville, I was part of a group that represented a waitress nightmare. Six of us descended on a hotel coffee shop, deep in conversation. No one wanted anything exactly as it was presented on the menu. Without meaning to be rude or difficult, we kept asking the waitress to change this or that, all the time continuing our animated conversation.

As she took our orders, the waitress was very friendly and patient. At the end of our meal I said, "My dear, this is going to be worth your while. We're all big tippers." The waitress said something I've never forgotten: "I'm not being nice to you for a tip. I don't care if you don't give me a tip. I just feel if we give you good service, your group will bring your business back to our hotel next year and not to the competition." That impressed me. I came back to San Francisco and wrote a letter to the hotel manager.

Dear Sir:

I am a motivational speaker, and I travel nationwide talking about good and bad service. I would like to congratulate you on all your staff. They were superb, but especially our waitress.

I related the tale, and finished:

Sir, I do not know what you did to motivate your people, but keep doing it. It works.

During the next eighteen months, I received no reply from the management of the hotel. In retelling this story, as I often did, I hinted that perhaps the waitress should have been a manager—she, I figured, would have the sense to acknowledge a compliment.

Then, at a Sales and Marketing Executives International Convention at the Fairmont Hotel in San Francisco, a woman approached me after my speech. "I am friendly with the management of that hotel," she said. "There is a new manager and that wouldn't happen now."

The next day, when I arrived at my office, there was a telephone message from a man in Nashville about the letter I had written eighteen months before. I asked my assistant to call and acknowledge his call, but before she could pick up the phone, it rang. He was calling to say, "I just wanted you to know we have new management, and I assure you that if you were to write a letter now, I would reply to it immediately. Please stop telling the story."

I told him I couldn't possibly stop because it was too good a story. However, I promised to add a new ending—that the new management phoned immediately when they heard the story. We laughed together.

Pretend You're the Customer

People who concentrate on giving good service always get more personal satisfaction as well as better business. How can we achieve better service? One way is by trying to see ourselves as others do.

Dr. Dru Scott Decker, in her book, *Time Management and Customer Satisfaction: The Other Half of Your Job*, tells how a group of public utility employees found out why their customers so often seemed confused and irritated. To seek the source of the problem, they went outside the building, then walked in, pretending they were customers.

"We really got into it," one employee reported later. "First we noticed there were no clear signs in the parking area telling people where to go. A tree had grown in front of our one sign. We stood in line and timed how long that took, and then guessed how it would feel to be sent to another window after waiting in the wrong line. We immediately saw how we could take steps to make our customers feel better about being there.

We suggested making a 'customer walk' part of the job of our bosses every month."

Handling Goof-ups

Even in the best-run business there will be mistakes and complaints. The secret is to learn from them and get on with business, rather than stopping to assign blame and punish the culprit. Making a customer feel bad, even when the error is probably his, doesn't make for good business.

Once I went to lunch with twenty-nine other people during a seminar in Southern California. We walked into the large, half-empty, Mexican restaurant at 12:15 and told the woman at the reservation desk we had a luncheon reservation for 12:30. She shouted angrily at us that our reservation had been for 12:00!

Now, we were giving that restaurant thirty customers. Even if she genuinely believed we were fifteen minutes late, we were still buying thirty lunches. Yet she insisted on chastising us loudly to "prove" the error had not been hers. We could have turned around and walked out, but that would have made us late for the afternoon session. After such an introduction, the best food in the world would probably be indigestible.

Still irritated, I went back to my hairstyling salon and told my staff, "I don't ever want to hear you tell a customer, 'You're late'—even though they sometimes are. It's better to say, 'We are a little behind schedule. Let's get moving.' That shares the responsibility rather than making anyone feel bad. The customer may have been stuck in rush-hour traffic. More likely than not, he is frazzled already, and to come in and be shouted at isn't going to help."

Take a Sniff

Mike Vance, known for his books *Think Out of the Box* and *Break Out of the Box*, talks about going over your business environment with your five senses—the feel, sights, sounds, smells, and tastes of what the customer encounters. After hearing

Mike describe "five-sensing," I discussed it with my employees. Then we walked through every area of our salon, observing everything the clients saw, heard, felt, smelled, and tasted. We asked questions like: Does the coffee always taste fresh? How can we get rid of the smell of the chemicals we occasionally use? Is this chair comfortable to sit in?

A dentist who specialized in children's care also heard Mike Vance's lecture. He went back to his office and walked around on his hands and knees, seeing what the experience of his office would be for a person the height of a child. Afterward he lowered the counter so even a very small person could see over it. He started asking children what they liked and disliked, and he worked with their ideas. He put photos of the dental hygienists on a board with a list of their interests, such as kite flying and skiing, so the child could choose the hygienist with whom he or she had the most in common. After giving his patients a questionnaire, this dentist found many were afraid of the instruments, so he explained exactly what he was going to do with each one. He also gave each young patient a photo of himself. He made going to the dentist a different experience and so much fun that all the children told their friends about him. In one year his practice grew so much that he needed several partners just to handle it all. His approach was a perfect example of how creative thinking and concentrating on serving clients can result in a better business and a substantial increase in income.

Five-sense your own environment. See what others see. Hear what others hear, taste what they taste, smell what they smell, as a stranger would. After people work in an organization for a couple of months, they no longer see their environment.

To learn these things about our businesses, we need feedback from our clients, customers, and employees. And occasionally we need to take a "customer walk," five-sensing our environment.

YOUR ASSIGNMENT:
The Impression Your Working Environment Makes

> **FRIPPICISM**
>
> *Customers want quality, value, speed, convenience, choice...and to be appreciated.*

Your best clients are the hottest prospects for your competitors. Answer the following questions to assess how likely you are to keep them with you:

1. The philosophy behind my organization is:

2. The statement we want to make in the business community is:

3. What do I see when I walk into my working environment?

4. What do I hear?

5. What do I smell?

6. What do I touch and feel?

7. How do the personnel relate to one another and to clients?

8. What things should be changed?

9. Whose help do I need to make these changes?

10. What specifically will I ask them to do?

11. My first step will be:

12. I will do this on (date):

Homework Assignment

Visit at least three other businesses similar to your own and "five-sense" them, writing down your findings.

CHAPTER 8

Talking Shop

FRIPPICISM

The future belongs to charismatic communicators who are technically competent.

In business today, straightforward communication is imperative. I'm not just saying that managers have to speak clearly to their staff. The lines have to be open from the top down and from the bottom up. I always ask executives one question: When was the last time you asked your assistant, your secretary, or anyone working under you what you could do to make his or her job easier?

Top managers who complain about poorly motivated employees should hear what I hear from the people under them. These administrative assistants and managers complain to me, "We're all revved up. We're ready to get going—but our boss is so disorganized."

"Why don't you go to your boss," I tell them, "and say, 'I'd like to earn the money you pay me by doing more than I do now. If you'll give me your priority projects each night before you leave, I'll work on them as soon as I come in the next morning, in that quiet time before you arrive.'"

Do you know how many people reply that they couldn't possibly say that to their boss? But a successful work environment encourages people to submit new ideas.

Boo Bue, an international trainer for Dale Carnegie (now retired), once told me about a superintendent of a large mill that had two problems with its production line: It couldn't keep the lines coordinated, and it had too many rejects. Management had never been able to solve these problems. The superintendent, using the creative thinking concept he had learned at Dale Carnegie seminars, got his workers together and said, "I need your help. We've got this production line that just isn't staying coordinated and causes too many rejects. We need your thinking. What can we do to solve the problems?"

After a while, an older man came to the superintendent and said, "I've got an idea I think would work." They tried it. In no time at all, the lines became coordinated, the rejects were reduced, and the company saved a thousand dollars a day. They had a recognition dinner for the employee. As the boss was patting him on the back, the guy confessed he'd gotten the idea five years earlier. Stunned, the boss said, "Five years! Why haven't you told us?" "You never asked me," the man replied. Now they have a suggestion box, a really big one.

I've told you to speak out whenever you think you have a Great Idea. You must also make it easy for others to share their Great Ideas with *you*.

Enthusiasm in the Ranks

When AT&T was going through huge changes, I spoke in Cleveland for Ohio Bell. The driver who met me at the airport was a walking press agent for the company. He'd been with them twenty-three years. At the offices, two secretaries matched his enthusiasm. One of them said, "The way our company is going, in two years [after divestiture], there probably won't be a job for us. But the experience of working for these people is so exciting we don't care if we lose our jobs." You can always tell what a company is like by talking to the people who may be thought of as being on the lower rungs.

When I met their boss, Jim Croll, I asked what he did to establish such loyalty, something that is a lot more difficult to do in a big company than in a small one. He told me every couple of months he sat down with his employees to have a "three-on-three" session. "I say, 'In managing you, what three things do I do that you like, that I should do more of? And what three things do I do that you don't like, that I should do less of?'"

Jim Croll was opening himself up for feedback, not criticism. Insecure managers often see any negative comments as a threat, an attempt to undermine their authority. But when managers genuinely seek feedback, they set the stage for their employees to say, "Here's what you're doing right, and here's what needs improvement. What can I do to help you?"

Your Source of Power

Power comes in two varieties. You have *position power* when you're the general, the boss, the CEO, the teacher, the parent, or the guard in charge of this cell block. You hold that power only as long as you hold the position.

You have *personal power* when people are drawn to you and eager to help you accomplish your goals. This power goes where you go because it is part of you. Think of politicians, businessmen, generals, even princesses. Some fade from sight as soon as they lose their titles. Others remain imposing and inspiring leaders and venerable "elder statesmen" without any official status.

The Role of Role Models

Without role models, we'd all still be sitting about in caves. One woman who provided a role model for me was Mary Sagan, owner of a successful laundry in San Francisco. When I first met Mary, I was twenty and she was forty. She was the only businesswoman I really knew when I first came to California. She was beautiful, always dressed well, and lived in an enormous and lovely condominium. She was constantly working to build her business, studying the *Wall Street Journal* and being proactive in her own investments. Seeing her, I wasn't envious, but I thought, "If she can do it, so can I." Like supportive employees and friends, a role model provides incentive.

One day when I had turned forty, I bumped into Mary on the street, and we made a lunch date. It was so nice to be a grown-up person and take my role model out to lunch. To my surprise and pleasure, Mary told me she had read about my progress and had always been sure I wouldn't "end up behind a chair." She said, "Once at my hairdresser's they were talking about you, so my ears pricked up. They said, 'Patricia Fripp doesn't take time for lunch. She doesn't even take time to go to the bathroom.' I was so amused because that was how I built my business, by wasting no time and eating my lunch at my desk."

The first time I discovered I was providing a similar incentive was when a young woman approached me and said, "I always try to emulate you. I bought a Dale Carnegie book because you recommended it. Carnegie said, 'Don't try to be like anyone else; just try to be like you.' Then I understood what you've been telling us—not to imitate other people, but to make the most of ourselves."

At that moment, I realized how important it is for women to have other women whom they can admire. I always try to provide role models for small entrepreneurs, especially women, who are entering the business world. Every one of us has this responsibility, to provide an incentive for other people to succeed. Every manager is responsible for modeling good business practices and personal integrity to their staff.

Three Good-Management Musts

Besides role modeling, managers share three primary responsibilities.

Delegating. Good management means delegating, and it also means always rewarding a job well done. Managers sometimes feel that they can do things better and faster, and they often can. But unless you take the time to train people to help you, you'll look around for help in a real emergency and discover everyone lacks experience. Teach your employees what you want and expect them to do. Then, to be sure they understand your instructions, ask them to tell you what they think they've heard. To reinforce your practice of distributing competence throughout the workplace, avoid "upward delegation." When employees bring you problems to solve, tell them to go away and return with three possible solutions.

Training. Don't invest more time in training people than they are willing to give you. It is a fact of life that some people are more ambitious than others. We often are disappointed when people don't live up to our expectations. To avoid disappointment, be more realistic and avoid disappointment. Decide who is prepared to grow and develop, and who isn't.

Rewarding. People need a paycheck, but when they can or will do only exactly what they are paid to do, they are doomed to mediocrity. But they can thrive and come alive and go the extra distance when you offer recognition and education.

Seven Minutes to Say "Thank You"

Staying in touch is as important as getting in touch. The first president of the National Speakers Association, Bill Gove, used to be sales manager for the 3M Company, and he wrote a lot of thank-you notes. One day someone was teasing him and said, "Hey, Bill, all you do is write notes all day long."

He said, "No, seven minutes a day. Everybody who does business with me hears from me at least once every three months, while my competition is calling on them, asking for their business."

Impressed by his story, I developed the habit of writing to my hairstyling customers as I now write and e-mail my speaking clients, thanking them for the opportunity to serve them. One of my clients, Hank Torchiani, used to come in at 7:45 in the morning once a month for the last eight years I had my salon. One day I dropped him this note: "Hank, have I told you recently how much I love waking up with you once a month?" (Naturally I sent that to his office, not his home. I'm not a troublemaker!) But the next time he came in he said, "Patricia, that was such a nice note, I'm keeping it in my box of treasures." He died in 1987, and I am very grateful I had communicated how much I enjoyed not only his patronage but also his friendship.

Remember, there are two kinds of people in the world to market to: those who know and love you and those who never heard of you. Most people spend a fortune trying to influence the latter, but the most important thing is to stay in touch with the people who already know you. (Some inexpensive ways to communicate with the people who don't know you yet are setting up a web site, writing journal articles, and being involved in community organizations.)

What a Personal Note Can Do

Letters of appreciation have to be genuine. They can't be formula public-relations pieces. Employees and customers spot phony, self-serving sentiments immediately and resent them even more than they resent being ignored. The anecdotes that follow are not intended to get you to turn out bulk mailings, just to emphasize the tremendous value of expressing your real gratitude.

Remember how former school teacher Susan RoAne got a career boost from Bea Pixa, who remembered a thank-you note? Another writer friend, Eleanor Dugan, told me about some unusual thank-you letters she once sent. "When a popular newscaster died, I suddenly realized how many public figures there are who become an important part of our lives, but we never bother to thank them. Then they're gone. So I sat down and sent notes to about a dozen people, mostly old-time performers who were no longer in the limelight, school teachers who had helped me, salespeople, librarians. If I didn't know how to reach them, I addressed them in care of organizations they probably belonged to like SAG (Screen Actors Guild) or found their names in their hometown phone books if they had retired. The amazing thing is that over the course of the next year, every one of those people, even the famous ones, replied with delightful and moving letters. I found out later that one of the people received my letter the same day he was fired from a job he had held for many years. I like to think my letter helped get him through that day, because his response was warm and upbeat."

A lot of times we just take for granted that others know how we feel, but more often than not, they don't. Not only do letters of genuine recognition work in business they work in personal life. I frequently write or e-mail my friends, telling them how much I appreciate their friendship, and they write back. Never underestimate the value of the written word for expressing what matters most. It's one thing to say it. It's another to take the time and trouble to write it. And very often you can say things in a letter you wouldn't say in person, because, face-to-face, you may feel a bit shy.

Having a successful life isn't just accomplishing great goals or having big exciting things happen. It also means paying attention to the little things—like thank-you notes—that can make such a difference in our daily life.

Interview Everyone You Meet

When I was behind a hairstyling chair in the financial district of San Francisco, I used to "interview" successful people. I'd ask them questions like:

- What were you doing when you were my age?
- How did you become the best salesperson for your company?
- What did you do for your little company that made some big company pay millions to buy it?

My brother teased me. "You ask such personal questions," he said. But in twenty-four years behind a hairstyling chair, no one ever said, "It's none of your damn business."

One day I said to my staff, "You are all interesting people. Why are you talking such drivel when you have so many fascinating people in your chairs? If you say they're not stimulating, maybe you're not asking them the right questions. I promise you that everyone can tell you the most amazing things."

Never decide someone can't teach you anything just because of your first impression. When I was fifteen, we had a client called Mrs. Dawson. She was large and intimidating and not very attractive. I tried to avoid her, but one day I was assigned to give her a 20-minute scalp massage treatment. So we talked and I found out what a really nice, kind, brilliant woman she was. She became my favorite customer. Once you get to know and like people, it's amazing how attractive they become!

What If You're Shy?

Does mingling with a roomful of total strangers make you uneasy? You're not alone. Most people are fundamentally shy, but the successful ones have learned to focus on all those exciting new people instead of the butterflies in their own stomachs.

Here's a tip for making the transition. If you go to networking events at organizations like your community Chamber of Commerce or a trade association, and you still classify yourself as a shy person, volunteer to be a greeter. You stand there with a label that says "Greeter" next to your name tag, and you have a specific job. "How do you do? I'm Chris Carter. Nice to meet you. Name tags are here. Food is there. How do you do? I'm Chris Carter. Nice to meet you." You've met lots of people and they've met you.

To help them remember you, wear your name tag up on your shoulder so people can see it when they shake your hand. (I have seen women put their name tags down on their handbags or in the most amazing places. Put it where they're not afraid they'll be sued if they look!) When people hear your name and read it at the same time, they're much more likely to retain it. Then they can look you up in the phone book.

At this same networking event, would you like people to ask you to give them a sales presentation on what you do? Shall I tell you how this can happen? Let me play a game with you. Pretend we are standing around the cheese dip at some community event.

First the routine way. You say, "Hi, I'm Chris, and I'm a professional speaker. Who are you and what do you do?" He replies, "Hi, I'm Rick Nelson. I'm a broker at Dean Witter." Without some effort on both your parts, the conversation may end right there.

But there's a simple way to make this common exchange into a more dynamic connection. When it's your turn, don't just give a job title or company name. That's what 90 percent of people do. Instead, reply with something interesting and provocative about your work, guaranteed to make them ask you, "How do you do that?"

One of my responses is, "I make conventions and sales meetings more exciting." Almost invariably, my new friend has to ask, "How do you do that?" And immediately I get to market myself: "You know how companies have meetings that are supposed to be exciting, and they're usually dull and boring? Well, I have some practical ideas I present in an entertaining way. The result is people stay awake, have a good time and get the company's message. My name is Patricia Fripp. I'm a professional speaker."

To which people usually say things like, "Oh, what do you talk about?" or "You know, we do have dull meetings," or "Hey, I heard a great speaker the other day." A conversation is established and soon I'm saying, "Does your company ever have speakers?"

YOUR ASSIGNMENT:
Business Communications

> FRIPPICISM
>
> *Life is a series of sales situations.*
> *If you never ask, the answer is*
> *invariably "no."*

Some daring and important questions I haven't yet asked are:

Of these questions, the one that could educate me the most is:

Homework Assignment

Schedule your seven minutes a day for business follow-ups. What time works best for you? How will you organize your correspondence list? (Tip: check the morning paper for names of people who should receive congratulations or condolences.)

CHAPTER 9

Friends and Lovers

> ### FRIPPICISM
>
> *My mother told me: "You will never meet anyone without faults. Marry someone whose faults you can live with." (I have stayed single.)*

Power in life and business comes from three things: who you are, who you are perceived to be, and who is on your side. This chapter is about the people you choose to have beside you.

You can't choose your family, and if you are happy with your relatives it's a cause for major celebration. However, you do pick your friends and lovers, and the world generally lumps you in the same category with them. Their simplistic assumption may not be entirely true, but it is an age-old adage that you are judged by the company you keep.

Clean the Closets of Your Life

Back in chapter 1, we talked about organizing closets. Now let's use closets as a metaphor for the various parts of your life. To become the person you are capable of being, you have to grow away from the people, habits, and thoughts that are keeping you from the life you want to lead. We'll talk about the habits and thoughts later. Let's start with the people.

The people who don't belong in your life fall into three categories:

1. People who are consistently unsupportive;
2. People with whom you have nothing in common;
3. People who are negative and depressing.

1. *The Non-Supporters*

People who don't support you, who even make a practice of belittling you and shooting you down in the name of "honesty," should be the first to go. To figure out who they are, first imagine a great victory. Perhaps you got a promotion, perhaps you lost twenty pounds, perhaps you ran five miles for the first time—imagine whatever a great win for you would be. Now imagine telling your spouse, your boss, your best friend, or your mother-in-law about your achievement. What do you think his or her automatic response would be? Would it be, "Hey, terrific, you can do it again"? Or "Hey, that's a fluke"? Or even an incredulous, "You?!"? If you are deliberately surrounding yourself with people who delight in demeaning you, getting the life you want will be much, much harder.

Of course, not everyone who fails to support us has evil intentions, either consciously or unconsciously. And criticism can be a powerful catalyst. Most of us can remember someone who, justly or unjustly, chewed our tails and made us reassess ourselves. Often this is a major turning point in our lives.

But one of the reasons we sometimes don't develop ourselves fully is that we choose to surround ourselves with people who tell us we can't do things. Even people who love us commit this error with the best of intentions. They don't want to see us hurt, they don't want to see us disappointed, or they are trying to protect us. (This happens a lot, I'm sure, in marriages and with parents.)

When I was thirty years old and had a well-paying job, my father told me not to go into business for myself. "Your staff," he warned, "will drive you crazy."

I said, "Father, I know my staff will drive me crazy. But you were in business for yourself when you were thirty. I'm thirty. I've got to do it."

My father hadn't spent any real time with me since I left home at eighteen. I was living on another continent. Although I went home on vacations and talked to my parents regularly, my father didn't know who I had become and what my capabilities were. The best thing for my relationship with my father was his coming to America and seeing me in my own environment. In our parents' minds, we never grow up, even when the roles reverse and we take care of them.

When you start planning what you want out of life, it is very important to discuss your plans with peers, mentors, and role models. But be aware that the people who are closest to you and have the best intentions may not necessarily give you the best advice. We want the ones we love to support us—but this may not always be easy for them to do.

Teachers play a strong role in shaping our self-image, for better or worse. Fortunately, a teacher's lack of support can sometimes stimulate healthy rebellion, an "I'll show you" response. The late Paul Mitchell wanted to be an actor. His mother, a hairdresser in Scotland, insisted he get his hairdresser's license first so he'd have a marketable skill to fall back on. Paul was tall, lanky, and rather clumsy. The owner of the hairstyling school told him he was too awkward ever to make it as a hairdresser. This didn't break Paul's heart because he hadn't wanted to be a hairdresser anyway. But, just to develop his confidence for the stage, Paul began entering hairstyling contests. To his surprise, he won most of them. Paul became famous as one of Vidal Sassoon's stars, then left to open his own school in New York. Paul Mitchell Professional Hair Care Products became one of the fastest-growing companies in the United States. Once Paul became famous, the owner of the school wanted to advertise that Paul was a former pupil. I'm sure Paul got great satisfaction out of saying, "No way."

Susan RoAne once told me, "Every time I talk to so-and-so, she makes me feel depressed. She has a way of talking about her own success that invalidates any success I may have." If you have known anyone like that, someone who invalidates your achievements and who makes your difficulties worse, redefine their role in your life. Why take the initiative to keep the relationship going if they don't make you feel good?

Trish Britt echoes my cautionary note: "Don't be discouraged by people around you. I think your friends have to be really positive people, productive people, people who are encouraging you, who know you, and who reinforce you. It's easy just to sit around and say, 'Oh, that will never work,' and 'You won't try hard enough.' You need positive people saying, 'Hey, that's a great idea!' and 'When do you start?'"

2. *The Nothing-in-Commons*

Some people get into what I call the going-to-dinner syndrome. You have dinner with John and Mary every fourth Friday; then you invite them back, though you really don't know why. You don't look forward to it. You don't enjoy yourself. You don't come away feeling expanded and elated, full of new ideas and insights as you do with other encounters. Every time you have dinner with John and Mary, you go home swearing you'll never do it again.

If you're not having a good time, you can be sure John and Mary aren't either. You need to say, "we've enjoyed playing cards with you for the last fifteen years, but we are reorganizing our priorities and staying home with the kids on Fridays." (Or "taking computer classes this fall" or just "we need more time alone together.")

If you spend three and a half hours one night a week socializing with people you don't enjoy being with and don't learn anything from, you waste four-and-a-half work weeks of your year. That alone can keep you groveling on your economic knees, not to mention the spiritual and intellectual aspects.

I have a good friend—a former good friend. We worked together years ago and had a terrific time, going to garage sales and flea markets every weekend. We loved it, and loved our friendship. It was very difficult for us to give this up because we'd been such great buddies. Now, understand, I'll always bail him out of jail. I'll make sure he never starves to death. But I will not invest an evening every couple of weeks to see him. Why? Because we have nothing in common any more. This does not invalidate the fact that we had many great times together. It does not invalidate the fact that we really loved each other. It just means we no longer have anything in common, anything that makes it worth spending time together. When you find your get-togethers with an old friend consist of nothing but reminiscences of happy times past, that there is no present, then you know it is time to move on. Please do yourself a favor: Say a fond goodbye to the friends and acquaintances that no longer belong in your life right now. Just enjoy the memories.

3. *The Downers*

The final person you must eliminate from your life is the negative, depressing one, the "victim" of the world. If you are going to adapt to changes in the future, you cannot surround yourself with victims. Often we get a virtuous thrill from the thought that we're saving someone, and it's great to do good deeds for altruistic reasons. But when the rescued doesn't benefit, even resents the rescuer's efforts, and the rescuer loses ground too, then it is an everybody-loses situation.

Let's consider how people often start their day. They go to work, go into the staff room, and hang around the coffee pot. There they listen to others talking about the miserable things in their lives. Many people automatically respond, "You think that's bad? You should hear what happened to me!" They're competing for being in the worst possible situation. One-downsmanship.

Starting your day this way has a devastating effect on the way you feel. It doesn't matter how energetic you are when you arrive at work if you get knocked down the minute you arrive. You're not going to have the energy to do your job. Make sure the people around you don't drag you down. Low self-esteem, yours or anyone else's, drains your time and energy.

My brother Robert Fripp, of rock band King Crimson fame, said in a press conference that this was the first band he'd been in where no one had a major drinking problem, drug problem, or woman problem. He said, "This is my fifteenth year as a professional. Do you know what it's like, for the very first time to work with people and not have to worry their personal problems will prevent them from getting on stage? Can you imagine going into a [business] office not knowing whether the people there can function because of their personal habits?"

What we often do, and shouldn't, is surround ourselves with people we know are unreliable, who constantly prove themselves to be unreliable. Sometimes we need to be in the midst of losers so we can feel in control. Sometimes we get a secret kick out of feeling superior to our companions: "Compared to him, I really look good." This may be a very comfortable way to live, but it stunts our personal growth.

That doesn't mean you can't accept the human frailties of others. But until people have committed themselves to positive change, you shouldn't carry the load for them. Find other people. You owe it to yourself.

Identify Your Cronies

Friends are great, but what you really want in life are some cronies. A crony is one step up from a friend, someone totally reliable. If you make a date to meet a crony at 6:15 in the morning and it is pouring rain, your crony will still be there at 6:14. I can honestly tell you that my women friends in San Francisco—my cronies—and our extended cronies in other cities get as excited about each other's success as we do about our own. It's good to have a forum where you can be proud of your accomplishments and feel support. It's equally valuable to be able to talk about disappointments and disasters with the same comfort. That's what cronies are for.

Being a close friend or crony doesn't mean you have to be in continuous contact. Because we all have such busy lives, my cronies and I get together irregularly, usually to celebrate each other's birthdays or holiday seasons. In honor of each other, we all dress up and look absolutely spectacular. At our dinners in each other's homes or in restaurants, we take turns describing what's happening in our lives. Everybody gets to hear. (Have you ever had the frustrating experience of going to a dinner party and talking only to the two people on either side of you?) At our get-togethers, all are complimented on their appearance, as well as their achievements. We all agree that each other's friendship is one of the most cherished things in our lives, and this knowledge helps us weather the storms everyone goes through periodically.

Now that we have e-mail to keep in touch, our contacts have gone international. I even write an e-mail column called Fripp News that I send all over the world. (Anyone who'd like to be put on the mailing list can e-mail me at PFripp@aol.com.) The great news about e-mail is you can be in touch with thousands of people, and it doesn't cost you postage and printing.

Bored or Boring?

A friend once said, "Sometimes I'm bored." I replied, "If you're bored, you're boring." I don't have enough time to spend with the fascinating, interesting people I already know, so I certainly don't have time to hang out with boring people. When you make decisions about what you want, be true only to yourself. This may be tough if you're in a major relationship, but do it.

"Love Me, Love My Hotdogging"

Another thing that amazes me, as a single person making decisions for myself, is how many couples feel they must do everything together. They're going to the opera but he hates it, or a football game, but she hates it. That's why you have friends, pals, and cronies. You'll have a lot more joy as a couple if you only do the things together that you enjoy. Go skiing or to the opera or the stadium with pals who love it so you can come back to your significant other and report what a great time you had.

For five years, I had a boyfriend who went rafting every single weekend during the summer. I went rafting once. I don't like being cold and wet. I don't think it's funny that supposedly sophisticated people like to throw buckets of icy water on each other. So I said to him, "I will never give you a bad time about your going rafting every weekend in the summer if you don't try to convince me to go with you again." Why shouldn't he enjoy a sport that he loves? Why should I be miserable when there are plenty of pleasurable things I can be doing? It is so nice to have peace and quiet, to lie back and read a thriller, to play with your computer, or to have extra-long hikes with your friends—whatever you want to do while your significant other is off doing what he or she loves, too.

If you are in any relationship—a romance, a marriage, or just a close friendship—if you can't entertain yourself while they do something they like, you may be a boring person.

Great Pickup Lines

There's much more to life than just business success. For one thing, we all need some romance. Love sends those endorphins coursing through our bodies and makes everything seem brighter. Who can enjoy a great career if they're terribly lonely when they get home?

How do you get romance in your life? The same way your great-great-grandparents did. You start by flirting! People used to marry for financial security and position in the community. These days, women can provide both of those for themselves and don't need to marry for them.

Ironically, the more successful, capable, and confident women become, the more intimidating they may seem to men. Today women keep their single names, and some married women don't wear wedding rings. In the old days, the men did all the asking, but today men can't be sure if a woman is available. No one wants to be rejected, so I work on the principle that women should let men know if they're interested.

First, an example of what not to do. When I still owned my hairstyling salon, I sued my attorney in small claims court and won. I walked down the steps of City Hall feeling good, and when you feel good, personally or professionally, it shows. Coming toward me was this gorgeous, well-dressed man. He asked, "How are you?" I said, "Terrific! How are you?" As I reached the bottom of the stairs, I turned around to check him out just as he turned around to check me out. And do you know what this stupid woman did, this woman who writes books telling people how to get what they want, this woman who goes all over the world saying, "Take charge of your life"? This stupid woman laughed and continued to her car. If I'd turned around and said, "How do you do, I'm Patricia Fripp, 38, and single," Who knows what adventures would have followed. Even if he'd been married, he would have been flattered!

Fortunately, both you and I can learn from my mistakes. I decided that day that I'd never overlook the opportunity to meet interesting men and women. I'd take the initiative, even if I was a little intimidated.

At that point, my true love had gotten his dream job and moved to Indianapolis. I hadn't dated for four months. I decided I was too luscious to go to waste.

"Goal for the week: find a boyfriend." But just writing this down, committing to it, and being passionate about it isn't going to get you anywhere until you get out and do something. So I told two friends, "we're going to go to the singles' event at the St. Francis Hotel. We'll meet at 18:00 hours and if I'm not in love by 20:00 hours, we're going home." (My friends say going anywhere with me is like a military maneuver.)

Unfortunately, at most of these so-called cultural events, the women have wonderful conversations with other women while the guys talk about sports. They never get together. At

8:15 p.m. that night, I was walking toward the elevator of the Sutter Street garage, as the doors were closing. Someone inside heard my footsteps, and I saw a hand hit the "Open" button. I stepped in and turned around to see what was attached to the hand. He was the closest thing to a Chuck Norris look-alike I've ever seen. (Chuck Norris is my fantasy lover.)

Immediately I thought to myself, "You've got to the third floor to let this guy know you're single." So I said, "I've just been to a terrible singles' event. You don't meet anyone at these events, do you?" This gave him the perfect opportunity to say, "I don't know. I've been happily married for sixteen years." He didn't. We chatted, reached the third level, and I stepped out. He got out too. His car was parked near mine, living proof there is a God. We chatted some more and exchanged business cards. "I'm going out of town for a week," I said.

"Call me when you get back," he said. I did, and we exchanged personal information. "We must get together for a beverage," he said. "Call me with a time," I said.

Two weeks later, no call. Now, I believe that life is a series of sales situations, and sometimes the biggest sale is to sell yourself. In a sales situation, the three steps are that you meet, you qualify, and you follow up...creatively. So I sent a postcard: "A girl could get very old and very thirsty waiting for your call." He called. We dated for nine months, and are still very good friends today.

So, practice harmless flirting. On an airport van, I sat next to two elderly gentlemen. One accidentally touched me and apologized. "That's okay," I said. I turned to his friend. "If I were you," I said, "I'd ask for equal time."

Those of you who are happily married may be saying, "but all this has nothing to do with me." My message to anyone who already has all the romance they can handle is: take the initiative in all parts of your life. Don't wait for opportunity to bite you on the bottom. You can flirt professionally, too, by making your availability known.

> FRIPPICISM
>
> *What fun you can have talking to strangers in elevators!*

Advice to the Lovelorn

During ratings week, I was on a talk show where they were discussing how to get your husband back after he's had an affair. My contribution was that there are two kinds of unfaithful husbands. One made a mistake and you want him back. The other is a rat and you don't want him back. A woman called with a tale of woe and asked my advice. I told her, "He was after your money. He's found someone else with more money. Dump him." After the show, she called again to ask if I did individual counseling. Of course I don't, so I referred her to my friend, therapist Luann Linquist.

Luann worked with her and gave her the identical advice. "But my job," Luann told me, "is to help her avoid repeating old patterns. That's why it costs $95 an hour."

The Personal Safety Issue

If you've seen or even heard of the movie *Fatal Attraction,* you're probably aware that danger can lurk in casual encounters and innocent pastimes. One day I met a masked gunman when I was running alone in the park. I chased him off with mace and bought a treadmill.

Chicago cop J.J. Bittenbinder gives seminars and talk shows about how to avoid being a victim. One of his stories may save your life. A woman working the night shift was waiting for a bus at 2:00 a.m. She noticed a suspicious-looking kid coming toward her, glancing around nervously. As he got near her, she stepped forward and said, "Don't I know your mother?!" He ran away.

Carol Everhart of the Rehoboth Chamber of Commerce in Delaware told me this story. One dark, rainy night she drove up to a luxury hotel. A fabulous Mercedes pulled in behind her and a well-dressed man got out. He said, "I hope they have room. If they don't, do you want to have a drink anyway?" Couldn't be more tempting, yes? A single woman and a handsome man in a fancy car? But Carol was tired and she passed.

She checked in and was directed to drive around to another building. However, she couldn't find the right building and returned to the desk. The handsome gentleman was still in the lobby. The desk clerk redirected her and she drove off again. When she found the right building, she couldn't get her key to open the outer security gate. Back she went through the rain to the main desk. The gentleman was still hanging around the lobby.

"You have to lean on the key, push, and turn," the clerk explained. (By now, you may have decided the hotel service was much less than what Carol was paying for!) She made her way back to the recalcitrant gate and had her key in her hand when the gentleman walked up the path behind her. "Isn't it nice they have room," he remarked pleasantly.

"I'm having trouble with the key," Carol commented.

He stepped forward helpfully. "Would you like me to try?" Now, here's your reality test. What would you have done next? Carol said, "Why don't you try *your* key?" He made an excuse and walked away. Carol returned to the desk and asked if the man had registered.

"No," the clerk replied. "He said our rooms are too expensive."

"Call the police," Carol said. "Something is seriously wrong." On this, her fourth visit to the registration desk, the clerk finally told Carol that it was possible to reach her room through an internal hallway without going back out in the rain!

The next morning, Carol read in the newspaper that a strangler was terrorizing the community, and the police were baffled about how he had been able to gain entry to so many locked hotel rooms. Carol was able to tell them when they arrived to interview her. (The night clerk had written up a report, but authorities hadn't been notified until the manager came on duty in the morning.) It turned out the Mercedes was stolen, just another device used by a very charming murderer to lull his victims into a false sense of security.

So protect yourself. Go with your gut feelings, and don't be foolishly polite because you fear hurting someone's feelings.

FRIPPICISM

You are never so right as when both of you see where you were both wrong.

Try Something Else

We are living in a stress-filled world. You recall that author Leonard Zunin spotlighted the importance of the first four minutes of any business encounter in his book, *Contact: The First Four Minutes.* He also urges people to give the first four minutes to their mates and family when they come home from work. Don't mention any problems, he says, until a pleasant mood has been established.

A speaker-friend, psychologist Susan Stephani of Hartland, Wisconsin, was on a program with me in Wisconsin. She told how one of her clients had complained, "I'm very stressed at work. My husband is very stressed at work. When he comes home in the evening, he comes into the kitchen and starts telling me about all the bad things that happened during the day.

Usually he starts nit-picking about something, I get mad at him, and we both blow up."

Stephani told her, "If you're doing something that doesn't work, do something else."

The next week, the woman came back and reported the same situation. And again Stephani repeated her advice: "If you're doing something that doesn't work, do something else."

The third week, the woman returned. "Last night, my husband came home and started to nit-pick."

The psychologist asked, "And what did you do?"

"Well, I couldn't think of anything else, so I started to tap-dance."

"What did he do?"

"He laughed. He asked me why I was tap-dancing, and I told him I was in a good mood. He said, 'Let's go out to dinner.' At dinner he told me he'd been under a lot of stress lately and was sorry he'd taken it out on me. 'I didn't get married to argue all the time,' he said. I told him, 'Nor did I.'" They came up with a pact that their first five minutes together at the end of the day would be devoted to letting off steam about work without any personal remarks. Then they would concentrate on each other and outside interests.

FRIPPICISM

If you've tried and tried, and it's not working, try something else!

YOUR ASSIGNMENT:
Friendship

FRIPPICISM

If the world were ending in ten minutes, every phone booth would be filled. Why wait? Start your phone list now.

---

1. Which friends make me feel better whenever I call them just to say hello?

2. Do I have the same effect on them? If not, why not? If so, what is it about me that makes my friends feel good about themselves?

3. If I had just met me, would I want to be my friend?

4. The last time I did something nice for someone with no thought of a "payback" was:

5. Do I need more support from the people in my life? If so, what communication skills do I need to learn or use?

6. Do I want to meet more interesting people? If so, how will I achieve this?

7. I am making the following appointments with myself for spring-cleaning my life.

Date

_____ I will clean out my clothes closet.

_____ I will clean out my work area.

_____ I will sit down with a pencil and paper, my address book, and calendar to analyze which of my personal relationships need refurbishing or no longer serve any purpose.

Homework Assignment

Say something true to the next three people you meet that will make them feel genuinely good about themselves.

CHAPTER 10

Working Smarter

> **FRIPPICISM**
>
> *Your best clients are also the hottest prospects for your competitors.*

The only thing I've ever wanted in business was an *unfair advantage* over my competition. That simply means I try to do everything a tiny bit better or more creatively or with more pizzazz. To work smarter, acquire an unfair advantage over your competition. It's really not hard.

Your Unfair Advantage

One of my clients, Gurn Freeman, who had just hired me to speak for FedEx, told me that earlier in his career his goal was to work for a moving company. He found 140 movers listed in the phone book. He called the first thirty-five and pretended he was relocating from Chicago to Phoenix. After every interaction with their salespeople, he made notes. What had they done well? How could they do it better? What had they done badly that they should learn from? How could they become so exceptional that they would have an "unfair advantage"?

Freeman's unfair advantage was that he noticed what worked and then modeled his sales strategies on what he had learned. (One technique practically guaranteed a sale: Before meeting with potential clients, he got materials from the local Chamber of Commerce in the city they were relocating to and used them as part of his sales presentation.)

To get to the top of your field and stay there, keep yourself fresh and excited by developing an unfair advantage. How?

- Do many small things slightly better than your competition.
- Do everything a bit better than you did yesterday, but not quite as well as you will tomorrow.
- Learn from every situation.
- Make decisions for the long term.
- Be creative.
- Invest time in "being prepared."
- Say "No" if you are not exactly right for the job.

Burton Cohen, General Manager of the Desert Inn in Las Vegas under Howard Hughes, once said, "If you want the possible done, you can call anybody. If you want the impossible done, call Judi Moreo." My friend Judi was in the special event and convention business in Las Vegas, and she definitely had an unfair advantage over her competition. For one client she created an attention-getting "living sculpture" for a convention display, using six fashion models wearing purple and silver on a rotating platform under shifting colored lights. And when the Desert Inn was opening a new wing, Judi took less than a week to locate 126 women who looked alike and then dressed them identically so they could line up at the entrance to greet guests.

Do you understand what an unfair advantage you have if people, your customers, think you can do the impossible? They never ask you how much you charge. If you're sitting there thinking "yes, but I can't *do* the impossible!" then you don't understand what the impossible really is.

The *impossible* is anything you can do that other people think they can't do. For me, the impossible is operating complex office equipment when my assistant is on vacation. There was a time I thought running a computer was impossible, until I learned how to do it. Most people are too modest. When you can do something—anything—that others regard as impossible, you've made yourself indispensable. Just let everyone know about it in a nice way.

Listen to Employees to Build Your Advantage

Nancy Albertson is a secretary at Sprint who came up with a $13 million idea. "I'm a big gal with big ideas," says Nancy. "The company said we needed to generate more revenue. It seemed so obvious to me that if you've sold a phone line to all the customers you can and you need more revenue, why not sell them a second phone line? We had gotten our teenaged daughter her own phone for Christmas—had the jack installed behind her dresser so she wouldn't see it until she had opened the box with the new phone on Christmas morning. So I submitted the idea through formal suggestion lines that they advertise, 'Give your teenagers their own phone lines for Christmas.'"

Her idea became a project called TeenLine that has made Sprint more than $13 million. "Okay, Nancy," I said, "I know they honored you at a banquet with your spouse and gave you a plaque, but don't you ever fantasize about getting just 1% of that $13 million?"

Nancy said, "I really make enough money, but it is such a privilege to work for a company that honestly cares what I think."

FRIPPICISM

There is nothing more revolutionary than a well-defined question.

Robert Fripp

If you want to improve your business, ask questions. And when you ask questions, *interview* people. Ask them: How do you see the problem? How long has this been going on? What would you do in this situation?

At the Nature Store, 60 percent of the business comes in the last quarter of the year, much of that from Christmas catalogue purchases. That means a huge bottleneck when everything has to ship at once. Sharon Currey Mills, vice president of catalogue orders, suggested having the guys on the floor help solve the problem: "Give them a few hours on company time to wander around," she said. Three men who make $10 an hour came up with some suggestions to solve the problem. "They were so proud," she told me. "They actually built a model of what the warehouse and distribution center should look like. They took me upstairs where they had it covered up, and they opened it with a big flourish. We used 95 percent of their suggestions."

"What," I asked, "would have happened if the vice presidents had solved the problem?"

"It would have taken at least fifteen hours at $100 an hour," Mills said, "and it probably wouldn't have worked because we'd have had no buy-in from the employees." Ask questions, and ask the right people!

How the Smart Guys Do It

The trouble with life is it is just too short to be good at too many things. You have to pick what you want to do and then do it well. Smart workers come in all colors, shapes, and sizes, but they have certain characteristics in common:

1. They share.
2. They make an effort.
3. They are persistent.
4. They are "lucky."

Let's look at how these four characteristics can affect work output.

1. They Share

At a seminar I attended, Jim Rohn suggested that poor people should take rich people to dinner. The idea is that if you ever get a chance to talk to a successful person, you'd better make the most of it. They may just let slip some of the reasons and ideas that made them successful.

Sharing ideas usually results in mutual goodwill and effective networking. I encourage salespeople, entrepreneurs—anybody with common interests—to set up their own mastermind alliances for brainstorming ideas or trading leads. I belong to the Continental Breakfast Club, a group of dynamic businesswomen who meet every two weeks to hear a speaker. It's a fabulous way to start the day. (Breakfast meetings cost less than lunch or dinner, have a built-in time limit, and send everyone off to work energized.)

"Not for Twice the Money"

Helping others to develop doesn't detract from you or create rivals. It helps you grow and creates supporters. For example, Evie Talmus worked for me when I first opened my salon in San Francisco. She worked hard, and on weekends started a little breakfast-in-bed delivery service. Bagels were her specialty. The business quickly grew. Eventually she opened a take-out food store, then a New York-style deli in San Francisco, and then was *in charge* of the restaurants for Western Athletic Clubs. When I went to her opening party, she said, "Patricia, I could not have done this if I hadn't worked for you and learned things from you that I use every day." In this same way, I feel I use ideas every day in business that I learned from celebrity hairstylist Jay Sebring in 1969, even though I am now in an entirely different business.

When Evie worked in my salon, she brought in a lot of customers for us by hitchhiking to work. (It was still considered safe then.) One day she accepted a ride and gave her sales presentation to a man who managed a beauty supply company. He offered her a job as a salesperson at double the salary I was paying her. She said, "You're going to think I'm crazy, but I love my job and haven't learned all I can yet. I'm not ready to leave, even for twice the money. I would be embarrassed to tell you what I earn because I'm turning you down."

Evie's refusal was not only loyalty to me, but an investment in her future because she was learning how to run a business. She left my salon with my encouragement and support, then applied what she had learned to her own business. When you help people grow, they help you grow. Now that Evie has gone on to become a successful therapist, and I'm in a new business as well, we still support each other.

Doing What Spiders Do

The spider-web concept involves getting out there and being visible in your community, not for a particular payoff but as a way of life. With the spider-web concept, you constantly promote and you constantly do, believing in the law of "sow and reap." Your actions will come back to you. For example, I refer business to many of my friends, who then wonder what they can do for me. I'm not doing it for that reason. I'm doing it because that's *what you do*! You must take an unselfish approach to promoting yourself.

Many of my friends ask me how I manage to get so much media and press attention. I always reply that for thirty years I've been an absolutely shameless, relentless self-promoter. By "shameless," I mean I am constantly marketing myself. I use a big "Fripp" logo on my stationery, I mention my name Fripp many times in speeches, I call my maxims Frippicisms, and I pass out buttons that say "I've been Frippnotized." I write articles and distribute *Fripp News*. And, sure enough, I get many business opportunities from people who have heard about me or read one of the articles—a perfect example of how the "spider web" works.

Making Bigger Pies

The reason the National Speakers Association is so successful is that Cavett Robert and Merlin Cundiff had the idea of a "bigger pie." The bigger pie means that, instead of everyone having smaller pieces of the same pie, the pie becomes larger because it is shared. When we work together, we increase the size of what we share.

2. They Make an Effort

It's true. Things aren't always easy. Many risks are inherent in striving for business success, especially starting your own venture. Coming from England as I have, I can honestly say America's business opportunities tower over those in other countries of the world. With energy, drive, and enthusiasm, you can accomplish wonders.

When I first came to America from England, I could bring only $500 with me. (I thought it was a fortune at the time, just as I thought everybody in America was rich.) I expected everyone here to be working exceptionally hard to attain the luxurious lifestyles my friends in England did not enjoy. But many people in America don't exert this above-average effort. I did, and although I would not say it's easy to be successful here, it is easier than it is in England.

One hairstylist friend of mine who has taken advantage of opportunities and put out above-average effort is Daniel Gianfrancesco, who has represented the United States in world hairstyling championships in about two hundred contests. At first, he placed second a few times, but since then he has placed first for years. Acclaimed as one of the best hairstylists in the world, Daniel practices sixty hours a week in preparation for a national competition. Why this total dedication? He says, "At thirteen I wanted to be not just a hairstylist, but I wanted to be the very best." He has worked overtime for his success in a world where few are committed to excellence.

When you have the urge to excel, you soon notice how few people dedicate themselves to the necessary level of commitment. What constantly dismays me even now, however, is how many people fail to take advantage of this country's opportunities. I'm certainly neither the smartest nor the best-educated person in the world. Yet, with my determined attitude and drive, I transformed my $500 into a successful hairstyling establishment and then into an ever-growing career in public speaking.

"You're Crazy!"

It takes hard work and concentration to keep a good reputation. And there are lots of people who think anyone who works that hard must be crazy.

When I used to lecture at barber schools, I said, "You have to be above average. That doesn't necessarily mean you have to be that much better, although it helps. It just means being a little nicer to your customers, being business-minded as well as promotion-minded." I have seen great hairstylists who didn't care about the people the hair was attached to. More important, I have seen good hairstylists with great personalities who succeeded where others who were better technicians didn't.

When hiring anyone—a speaker, doctor, dentist, or hairstylist—if you find two people of similar ability, you're going to return to the person you like. If you can make the things you have to do (like having your hair cut or your teeth fixed) as pleasant as possible, life is going to be better. Anyone providing a service to people needs to do more than the next person.

3. They Are Persistent

Someone asked Bud Friedman, founder of The Improv Comedy Clubs, "Is there such a thing as natural talent?"

"Yes," he said, "but there's no such thing as overnight success. Jay Leno is a natural talent, but he used to drive four hours from Boston to New York City to try to get five minutes on an open mike at the Improv. I finally put him on, not because I thought he was any good, but because he'd driven so far. He was naturally talented and he got better, but it still took him fifteen years before he started hitting the jackpot."

As I say to many who tell me they want to become speakers, *You probably don't lack the talent, but you may lack the patience.*

The Way to the Boss's Office

In my own case, because of my father's business career in England, I developed an attitude that persistence pays. In the 1920s, my father supported himself as a farmer's hired hand. He worked seven days a week and was paid six shillings a day (less than a dollar), plus an extra shilling for Sundays. He worked hard for several farmers at this wage, living with the hired hands in barn lofts and similarly close quarters.

One day my father spoke to a local businessman and told him he wanted desperately to work in an office. "Learn shorthand and typing," the man advised. My father wanted to know how that would help him. "It isn't the skills themselves," the man replied. "It's the fact that they will get you into the boss's office."

Determined, my father went to night school for two years to learn these skills. By day he pumped gas to pay for his education. Finally, he got a position in a real estate office for twenty-five shillings a week (just over two dollars). He was an eager man and a fast learner. The two partners were glad to have him aboard.

However, the partnership soon began to dissolve. The owners did not know how to repay the three or four hundred pounds they owed to various creditors. Although my father had only five pounds in the bank, he offered to assume responsibility for their debts if the partners gave him the business.

The feuding duo liked this idea, so off they went, leaving my inexperienced father to deal with the mass of creditors and bills. Being an honest, hard-working man, my father went to each creditor and said, "I've taken over this business and I certainly owe you money. I haven't a lot of experience. If you sue the old owners for the money, you won't get it because they haven't got it. Take a chance with me, and I'll repay you as soon as I can."

The creditors all agreed. That was my father's beginning. Within a few years, he had not only repaid the debt, but made one of the biggest land deals in the county. With luck (which, as you know, comes mostly from taking advantage of the opportunities your problems present) and with hard work, he made it past many tribulations including the war-torn English economy to become a prosperous businessman. He remained a successful real estate agent for more than forty years.

With my father as an example, I saw my success as just a matter of time and effort. I have learned that if you stick to a good plan of action, you largely account for your own success. You make your own luck.

4. They Are "Lucky"

For many years, Max Gunther, author of *The Luck Factor*, has studied lucky people. He's found specific traits that characterize those regarded as lucky. Gunther compares them to a spider: "A spider strings many lines to catch passing flies and the bigger her web, the better she eats. So it is with those who would catch good luck. In general...the luckiest men and women are those who have taken the trouble to form a great many friendly contacts with other people."

This is essential in business. Joseph Baim, then president of Markham Products, Inc., the company I demonstrated for when I owned my salon, was attending a packaging convention at a seaside resort. At the time, there was a very popular product called PPT that had been designed for the Redken Company. It was a marvelous hair conditioner, and no matter what product line people carried in their barbershops or beauty salons, they always had some PPT because it worked magic. For years, Mr. Baim had wanted to find someone who could make a product as good as PPT.

During the convention, the friendly Mrs. Baim struck up a conversation with a woman on the beach, and the two decided to go out to dinner that night with their husbands. It turned out the woman's husband was the man who had invented PPT for Redken. He now had his own manufacturing company and was free to make a rival product for Baim. This may seem like pure luck, but Mrs. Baim's characteristically outgoing personality made the resulting success possible. Friendly interest in other people works wonders.

FRIPPICISM

Whether you work for a company or yourself, you have to be memorable.

In Gunther's words, "[Lucky] people make themselves known to many other people, usually without thinking about it. They're gregarious. They go out of their way to be friendly. They talk to strangers, they're joyous meeters and greeters. If they sit next to someone on an airplane, they start a conversation. The guy who sells them their morning newspaper is more than just a face." People of this type put the odds in their favor. They lay the groundwork to have luck come their way.

And luck, as you can see, is a combination of the other three characteristics of smart workers: sharing, effort, and persistence.

Blow Your Own Horn

At a meeting of the National Association of Fleet Administrators, I met a man who had saved his company $250,000 the previous year. The only way his company found out about it was that he asked his supervisor to sign a form from his professional association so he'd be eligible for an award. This man's attitude was, "I was only doing my job."

Yes, you're only doing your job, but when you're doing it superbly, make sure people know about it! You have to be an absolutely unashamed, relentless self-promoter, even if you do it subtly. A man sitting next to me on a plane told me about an incredibly dull 18-page presentation he had written, even though he was passionate about the subject. Fortunately, he took it to a young woman in the company's communications department. As a favor for a colleague, she created slides, graphs, visuals, and cartoons on her own time. Her material was so dynamic that her colleague's speech was a great success. Word of her talents got around, bringing her international recognition. Today she supervises both their internal and customer presentations. That's not why she did someone a favor, but the right people found out who deserved the credit.

Although it should go without saying, let me spell out the lesson: If someone helps give your business an unfair advantage, put that person in a position to do it more often!

The "Secret" of Success

I've always loved what I do for a living the way some people love their hobbies and recreation. People who work smarter have found a passion that goes way beyond any paycheck. You may work hard eight hours a day, but you'll rarely achieve anything exceptional in that time. Most of my working life I've worked twelve hours a day minimum, six or seven days a week, but because I love what I do, I've never felt put upon. That doesn't mean I've loved every *aspect* of what I do, but the total picture is irresistible.

Carole Kelby has that passion. She sold $15 million worth of homes in a lean year in which the average home sold for $100,000. I know from meeting people who worked with her or who lived in her area that many thought she was the exclusive

Realtor for a particular section of town. That wasn't true, but it was the perception. Years later, I asked her how she did it.

"Once I listed the home of a gentleman who was buying his next house directly from the builder. That meant no money for me on that part of the transaction. However, I realized that if he paid me a commission for selling his house, he wasn't going to qualify for a loan. There was only one thing I could do. 'Get out a pen,' I said, 'I'm going to tell you how to sell your present house yourself.'" He was astonished and wanted to know why on earth I'd help him avoid paying me a commission. "I guess you call it the cost of doing business," I told him. "You don't get paid for everything you do."

The man called her the next day. "Do you know what I do for a living?" he asked.

"Yes," she said, "you work in personnel for a big company."

"I'm in charge of personnel," he told her. "We just merged with another company, and we're hiring 3,000 new people. Many of them will be relocating, and they're all yours."

Carole laughs. "At the time, I thought, what if he's lying and he only sends me a hundred?"

FRIPPICISM

When I wear a hat, many wonderful people I don't know initiate conversations.

Stand Out in the Crowd

Remember, there is no point going anywhere if people won't remember you were there. What can you wear, say, or do that will make you noticed without being notorious?

I happen to be famous in San Francisco and at the National Speakers Association for my hats. I happen to like them, and it is part of my overall marketing strategy to be noticed. Often they work for me at large events because I'm the only one with a hat. People are sparked to start a conversation: "Oh, I like your hat." Or "My mother used to wear hats."

And, I say, "Yes, they make nice people like you talk to me. Hello, I'm Patricia. Who are you?" That gives me an unfair advantage.

It is a violation of traditional etiquette for men to wear hats indoors, but I met a young man at a gathering in Denver who'd devised a great attention-getter of his own. When I was chatting with him, I said, "Oh, your lapel pin is upside down. What does it say?" I reached over and turned it around.

"I always wear it upside down," he said, "so people like you will notice and turn it around to read it." This gave him his unfair advantage. See what I mean? Being "unfair" means doing one small thing better, more creatively, more innovatively than your competition. It can be high-tech, low-tech, no-tech, no-cost, as long as it's creative.

YOUR ASSIGNMENT:
Working Smarter

> FRIPPICISM
>
> *Don't concentrate on making a lot of money. Concentrate on becoming the kind of person people want to do business with.*
>
> Arthur Henry Fripp

Can I Succeed in Business?

1. The most important lesson I have learned so far in life is:

2. My most recent lesson was:

3. Something valuable I've learned from observing others is:

4. When I walk into other people's businesses, do I frequently learn something new?

5. How often do I ask my manager what he/she thinks?

6. How often do I ask people around me what they think and know?

7. How many books have I read in the past month? The past year?

8. How many informational tapes have I listened to in the past year?

9. How many seminars have I attended in the past year?

10. What do I do so I can grow every day?

11. Who is the most surprising successful person I know? Why?

12. What can I learn from this person?

13. What is the best decision I have made about my career?

14. The process I went through to make this decision was:

Do I Get the Most Out of My Job?

1. Do I have enough drive?   YES   NO

2. Do I accept responsibility cheerfully?   YES   NO

3. Do I believe success is not an accident?   YES   NO

4. Do I welcome and evaluate new ideas?   YES   NO

5. Do my mistakes give me new insights and help me grow?
   YES   NO

6. Do I believe my neighbor's lawn only *seems* greener?
   YES   NO

7. Do I truly believe my future is my own responsibility?   YES
   NO

8. Do I realize the world definitely does *not* owe me a living?
   YES   NO

9. Have I accepted that no one is going to come and rescue me so I better do it myself? YES NO

10. Am I as careful as I want to be with my finances? YES NO

11. Do I have a lifestyle that keeps me physically and mentally fit? YES NO

12. Do I regularly evaluate my progress and adjust my goals accordingly? YES NO

13. Do I accept that everything worth having has a price tag of some sort? YES NO

14. Do I remember the good things others have done for me? YES NO

15. Do I understand and make friends with the people I work with? YES NO

16. Do I look for the best in people? YES NO

17. Do I consider self-improvement a priority? YES NO

18. Do I take time to relax? YES NO

19. Do I consider work an exciting and rewarding privilege, not a dreary chore? YES NO

Do I Give My Best to My Job?

1. Do I take enough time to get all the facts? YES NO

2. Do I take enough time to listen? YES NO

3. Do I take enough time to think and plan?   YES   NO

4. Am I thorough?   YES   NO

5. Do I finish what I start?   YES   NO

6. Do I take orders as cheerfully as I give them?   YES   NO

7. Can I usually be concise?   YES   NO

8. Am I good at prioritizing?   YES   NO

9. Do I always admit my mistakes and then correct them?
   YES   NO

10. Am I punctual?   YES   NO

11. Am I neat?   YES   NO

12. Am I courteous?   YES   NO

13. Am I tolerant?   YES   NO

14. Am I patient?   YES   NO

15. Do I keep my promises?   YES   NO

16. Do I believe good manners are good business?
   YES   NO

17. Am I enthusiastic?   YES   NO

18. Do I avoid gossip?   YES   NO

19. Do I speak clearly and convincingly?   YES   NO

20. Do I look, listen, and learn daily?   YES   NO

21. Do I go find the answer when I'm not sure?   YES   NO

22. Do I set a positive example for others?   YES   NO

23. Am I careful to share the credit?   YES   NO

24. Do I cooperate with the people I work with?   YES   NO

25. Am I good at making others feel important?   YES   NO

26. Do I always try to help my superiors?   YES   NO

27. Do I always try to help those I supervise?   YES   NO

28. Do I control my temper?   YES   NO

29. Do I always appear enthusiastic, even when I don't feel like it?   YES   NO

30. Am I always willing to go "the extra mile"?   YES   NO

Homework Assignment

List all the bosses you've ever worked for and what you learned from them, good or bad. (You can learn something from everyone, if only a pitiful example of what not to do!)

CHAPTER 11

Make Success a Habit

FRIPPICISM

*Success is not whom you know,
but who wants to know you.*

Our habits are part of us, built up like the layers of a pearl from our own juices. They can either provide a lustrous shield against adversity—or an imprisoning shell of our own making. Just a few habits can make a big difference in both how we handle and how we project ourselves. What new habits do you want to acquire? What old habits do you want to change?

Habit or Commitment?

Remember how Ken Blanchard, coauthor of *The One Minute Manager*, describes the crucial difference between "interest in" and "commitment to"? He continues, "People who want to develop new habits should notice how they describe their goal. Do they say they are interested in it? Or do they have a commitment?"

If you are interested in your health, then you go to the gym when the weather's nice and your friends are willing to go. But if you have a commitment, you go whether you feel like it or not, no matter how late you got in the night before, and whether your pals are going with you or not.

Are you just interested in achieving your goals and developing good work habits? Or are you *committed*?

Five Steps to New Habits

You have a choice. You can improve by experimenting with new ideas. Or you can continue doing comfortable things that don't work. If you choose the former, here is what it requires.

1. *Make up your mind.* Be committed to making the change. For instance, you decide to be on time each morning rather than constantly offering excuses about what caused you to be late. You analyze the actual reasons for repeated lateness and take specific actions: getting up and/or leaving the house at a different time; changing the car pool route or rules; taking a different means of transportation; taking an earlier train; preparing the night before by laying out clothes, packing lunches, etc.; negotiating an end to delaying tactics of spouses, children, or co-carpoolers.

2. *Describe your new behavior in writing.* Not only does this give you a record of what you're doing, but the physical act of writing something down and then reading it back forms the first neurochemical thread of axons in your brain that will eventually form the permanent mental chain called habit.

3. *Share it.* Announce the change publicly. Tell the world or at least someone in your support system. Changing habits is never easy, and you need all the boosters you can get. (Avoid the "friend" who says, "Aw, come on, cheat a little." If you run across someone this insensitive, reply in an indignant voice, "Why should I cheat myself?")

4. *Act immediately*—or as soon as possible. If you decide you will stop complaining, start not complaining today, not tomorrow. Or when you go home at the end of the day, resist

temptation to complain to your spouse, roommate, or children. Act immediately on whatever you have decided.

5. *Persist for three weeks.* Remember, that's how long it takes to form a new habit. Invest the time to ingrain your new habit, to get your subconscious acquainted with the new place you've put your wastebasket. There's another reason for the three-week timetable: It's a lot easier to try something different and uncomfortable when you can see an end to it, a definite time limit rather than a dreary chore stretching on forever. The "carrot" of completing those twenty-one days keeps you going. At the end of that time, either your new regime has become a habit or its benefits are so overwhelming that you will be eager to continue it until it does become a habit.

The Railroad Tracks of Life

In *Make Your Mind Work For You*, my friends Joan Minninger and Eleanor Dugan say that "habits are like railroad tracks. You lay them down with a lot of effort so that later you can get where you want to be, smoothly and easily."

Continuing the railroad analogy, you sometimes find a particular station or spur line is no longer useful. Then it's time to lay new track. "Brains don't learn to get results," says psychologist Richard Bandler, "they learn to go in directions." Which direction do you want your tracks to go? Surely, planning your life is as important as planning a travel itinerary.

Minninger and Dugan recommend the use of playful techniques rather than self-harassment to overcome resistance when you decide to change a habit. For instance, you can tell yourself, "Every time I write an appointment or phone number directly in my book instead of on the back of an old envelope, I'll draw a little silly face next to it." Even if you choose not to draw the comic face, you have begun the change you want to make.

Remember, it took a lot of effort to create the habits you have now. They represent your personal power. You can decide to use that power to do something else, to leverage yourself to where you want to be.

A Sure Sign of Commitment

Alan Cimberg, a senior statesman at the National Speakers Association and a top sales trainer for forty-five years, got his first sales job selling encyclopedias door to door one summer. "That's the best selling of all," he says. "I think if a man walked in and said he had experience selling house to house, I would hire him on the spot. Do you know why? Because house-to-house salespeople have to be committed to withstand the frequent rejections they face many times a day. That's the formula: What they were, they will be."

Even if you didn't have that kind of commitment in the past, you can develop it now. What you make yourself now, you will be.

Practical Uses for Ego

When I was thirty-five, my life was going pretty well and I wanted to do something to prove to me I could do anything. I took up running, even though I've never been athletic. I am a short-term project person, and I decided running a half-marathon starting from scratch would be very good long-term discipline. With running, it's easy to measure your progress.

To get support for long-term goals, it helps to share them. I ran with Bert Decker once in a while, and I'd call him every Monday to report how far I'd run the week before. I'm sure he didn't care, but my ego helped to reinforce my discipline. If I'd run fifteen miles last week, it would be mortifying to report that I'd run only three this week. I used someone else to help me be committed and stick to my goal.

Do You Want to Be Famous?

At conventions I'm treated royally, but then I can go home and be a real person. (Sometimes a prospective client says,

"I never heard of you." I reply, "If you had heard of me, you wouldn't be able to afford me!")

My brother says, "Why would anyone want to be famous? Can you imagine what it's like to be gawked at and followed everywhere you go?" Celebrities rarely lead happy lives, despite the solace of the extra income that their status sometimes brings.

The esteem and admiration of your colleagues and being exceptionally well known in your business community or professional association are commendable goals, but I recommend avoiding the kind of fame that has the papparazzi going through your garbage for scandalous tidbits.

Who Owns the Future?

The future belongs to charismatic communicators who are technically competent. Does that describe you?

YOUR ASSIGNMENT:
Choosing Your Habits

> FRIPPICISM
>
> *Small additional increments are transformational.*
>
> Robert Fripp

Which of my current habits help me?

Which habits *don't* help me?

What new habits do I want to acquire?

Which habits will I get rid of?

CHAPTER 12

Finding Time

FRIPPICISM
Your future is the only time you have left.

If you want to take charge of your life, you have to take charge of your time. Whether time is your friend or foe depends on how you use it.

Clichés That Work

The problem with clichés is that, although they often contain momentous truths, they become almost meaningless with repetition. You probably hear information every day that could turn your life around, but you ignore it simply because you've heard it so many times before without it altering your life. Fortunately, sometimes something "clicks" and the cliché changes our lives forever.

Spending Time Like Money

Too many people waste their time and their money in the same sorry way, going for every bright trinket they come upon so there is nothing left for the important things. The average

American family spends approximately seven hours a day watching television!

Of course, there are some wonderful television programs, but we need to make conscious choices about what and when we watch. Don't become a couch potato. Ask yourself: Is this program improving me as a person? Enriching me? (Don't forget that relaxation counts as enrichment and that a few minutes of laughing at a funny TV program may prevent lengthier, more expensive therapy.) Is this program helping me toward my goals? Is there anything else I would rather be doing right now?

> **FRIPPICISM**
>
> *It's better to do something for nothing than nothing for nothing.*

No Time for Planning

Some people feel planning requires rigid scheduling with no room for experiments, side trips, or pleasure. In *Make Your Mind Work For You*, Joan Minninger and Eleanor Dugan compare nonplanners to jellyfish, "drifting back and forth between existence in the water and extinction on the shore. Farther out in the ocean are the whales and dolphins, cavorting, playing, enjoying themselves immensely, but always following their migration patterns, their plans. Is the life-plan of a whale really more restrictive than the drifting of a jellyfish?"

How to Create Time

One hour a day every day adds up to nine 40-hour weeks each year. Most of us use the excuse that we don't have time to read, exercise, or be with our families. But if we got up half an hour earlier every day, we would create four-and-a-half working weeks a year. Eliminating just fifteen wasted minutes each day gives you more than eleven extra days each year. Good time management techniques create extra time in which to achieve your goals.

Many people say time is money. That's true to a certain extent, with one important difference. You can put money in the bank and draw the money itself back out, plus interest. But once you've invested an hour, the hour itself is gone. All you have is the interest. This interest, however, is what life is all about. When you spend time on training, learning, and developing yourself, you get it back many times over.

Efficiency and Effectiveness

Don't confuse activity with accomplishment. Choose the best ways to use your time instead of racing around in a circle. Management expert Peter Drucker sees a big difference between being efficient and being effective.

- Efficiency is doing things right.
- Effectiveness is doing the right things.

There are two reasons why people don't manage their time well. Either they have not been taught proper techniques or they are not motivated. For example, a person may say, "I'm going to wait until I have more time to get organized" or "Time management doesn't work for me. I always lose my list." Sometimes you even hear, "I don't have time to do it correctly right now, but I'll come back later and fix it"—as if the future held limitless time to undo and redo something done poorly. If you ever offer excuses like these, then your problem is motivation.

The ABCs of To-Do Lists

Every time you think of something you need or want to do, write it down. At your daily organizing session, these notes become your To-Do List for the next day, the next week, the next year.

Now take your To-Do List for tomorrow and turn it into an ABC List. You should be able to divide everything you want To-Do into three categories:

- The A's: major aspects of your job, business, or personal life
- The B's: not as urgent
- The C's: bothersome but must be done eventually

Each day I take my To-Do List and code it with A's, B's, and C's. This helps me make sure I don't spend all of my time with the smaller, time-consuming C jobs when I should be working toward A goals. Your ABC To-Do List can be the most useful tool you have at your disposal.

Jot down everything you have to do or would like to do the next day. Of course, you rarely think of things in their order of importance. That's why you go back and decide which things are most important, have the highest payoff, bring you closer to your goals, the things that are going to make you happy and successful. Put a big A next to those items. These are the items you should do first.

Write a B next to the things that are important, but are not high priority.

Then anything that is nice if you get around to doing it becomes a C priority item. Do not do C items at the time of day when you are most energetic.

First thing in the morning you should do the icky things, the priorities you're not crazy about. Otherwise you will allow your other work to expand throughout the day, and at six o'clock you'll be able to yawn and say, "What a hard worker I am. Too bad I didn't get around to calling that unhappy customer."

When you complete an item on your schedule, cross it out. That makes you feel good. Attach the sheets of your ABC's To-Do pad to your calendar so your weekly and monthly schedules are also with your ABC pad. Before the end of each day, plan the next day.

Periodically recheck your checklists. Time management expert John Lee suggests we do After Action Analyses of everything we do. At the end of the day or after a major activity, check to see whether you have left anything important off your To-Do List. Decide how you can prepare better next time.

Planning Ahead

At the end of each week, take your calendar and plan the following week. If you like, you can have separate To-Do sheets for each day of the week—Monday, Tuesday, and so forth—and jot down items as you think of them. Then consolidate these lists onto your weekly list.

Many people say their high-priority items involve such big projects that they never get around to doing them. If this happens to you, find an hour of peace and quiet to think, plan, organize, and do. Sometimes that may seem impossible, but one uninterrupted hour is the equivalent of at least three hours with interruptions. (Even four 15-minute segments are far less effective than that one solid hour.)

Don't Overbook

Did you write in an activity for every single space during your waking hours? That's unrealistic! Make plans that allow time for unexpected emergencies. Time management techniques fail when the people using them unrealistically overbook their time. Then the first time an emergency comes along they get flustered, blaming the techniques instead of their over-optimism. Be realistic in your planning.

People tell me they have problems with starting projects but not finishing them. If that happens to you, perhaps you are being unrealistic with your schedule. Do not write eight pages of To-Do items for Monday. That's far too many. You shouldn't be working with more than two pages. To-Do pads are like goals: If you plan them too big, they don't work.

Play with Blocks...of Time

Many executives find that using a time log helps them reserve larger blocks of time for projects that can't be picked up and put down easily. Even if you have an open-door policy, this is essential for high-priority items. Schedule yourself for at least one uninterrupted hour a day. Early in the morning is good if you're a morning person—at home before the family gets up or at the office before anyone else arrives—but some people prefer lunchtime at the office, before dinner, or late at night after everyone is in bed.

Your Ideal Day

Imagine your ideal workday. Would you get up an hour earlier? Would you schedule something before beginning work (exercise, meditation, socializing, planning)? Would you set aside time during the day for phone calls, for errands like going to the bank and post office? For personal relationships? For reading? For watching television or listening to music? Your life will never be perfect, but unless you have a vision of perfection, you don't know what to work toward.

Your "Ideal Working Day" is your model for the future. How can you turn it into a reality? Start by applying the following time blasters.

Decide What's Important

Discover what is vital and what is trivial. This is known as the 80-20 rule: 80 percent of the value is accounted for by 20 percent of the items, while 20 percent of the value is accounted for by 80 percent of the items. Learn to concentrate on the high-value 20 percent items.

If time is money, you should have an idea of what it costs you to do different tasks. For example, if you make $25,000 a year, your time is worth about $12.50 an hour, based on a forty-hour week. When you make $50,000, your time is worth $25 an hour. If someone making $6.00 an hour can do a task 80 percent as effectively as someone making $25 an hour, maybe he should do it.

Make the best use of your time. Give the right kind of time, the high-energy time, to the important tasks, your A projects.

Know What You Shouldn't Do

When I wrote the first edition of *Get What You Want*, my staff wanted a party to celebrate the book. (Frankly, they liked any excuse to celebrate anything.) I said, "Fine; if we have a party, will you do all the work? Will you decorate the hall, hang up the streamers, blow up the balloons, invite the people, chop up the cheese, pour out the wine, and clean up after it?" "Yes, Patricia!"

My staff was very much like some of the people you work with. Once the enthusiasm wears off, they're not so excited. So again I confirmed. I said, "Are you absolutely sure that, when the novelty has worn off you will still want to do all the work, hang up the streamers, blow up the balloons, and so forth?" Again, the affirmative. Two days before the party, I was walking out of the salon through a big hall outside our business that we were allowed to use for parties. My favorite employee was up at the top of the stepladder, blowing up balloons, and I knew she would be there until probably nine o'clock that night. I thought I should stay to help her, teamwork and all that. But, fortunately, in a moment of insight one of my own speeches came to mind:

FRIPPICISM

There is no point doing well what you shouldn't be doing at all.

My job had been to write the book. My job had been to negotiate with the publisher. My job had been to think of ways to sell the book. My job was not to blow up balloons. And I had had their agreement and commitment to do the work. Even though my friends tease me that, with all my hot air, I could be the best balloon-blower-upper in northern California, I left to work on the projects only I could do for our business.

Learn to Say "No" by Saying "Yes"

Unassertive people say "yes" when they really want to say "no" because they don't want to hurt the feelings of others. Ironically, however, they often cause more ill will in the future. Fortunately, there is a way to say "yes" at the same time you say "no."

My salon in San Francisco was in the same building as the Chamber of Commerce. Naturally, I was a member. One of the executives asked me to run a luncheon once a month for their volunteers. I said, "No. Because of my travel schedule, I won't be there often enough. However, let me tell you what I can do. Once a year I'll give a free talk to rev up your volunteers. That way you use a talent of mine that most of your other members don't have." I was saying "yes" and "no" at the same time: "no" to the original request, but "yes" to supporting the organization.

Recently, I was asked to be on the Board of Advisors for the Advanced Toastmaster Club. "No," I said, but countered by offering to send them articles for their Toastmaster newsletter from my on-line, *Speaker Fripp News*. It was something of value to them that takes me no time. (If you want a copy, e-mail PFripp@aol.com.)

Debbi Steele, who used to be sales manager for several small San Francisco hotels, was exceptionally active in the business community and in the hospitality industry. Debbi is a generous woman with her time and knowledge. She was always taking time away from her desk to talk to people who wanted to know about the hotel industry, then working late at night to catch up. I told her about my "no/yes" strategy.

One day when we were running she said, "Fripp, you'll be proud of me. I took your advice. A young woman asked me to have lunch with her so I could tell her about the hotel business. I said "no" to her invitation, but gave her two choices. One, she could run with me at 6:30 in the morning and we could talk. Or, two, she could spend the afternoon in my office, working for me for nothing, stuffing envelopes and answering the phone. We would talk while we were working. The young woman decided on the second choice, and afterward thanked me profusely. She now understood what it was going to be like working in a sales manager's office." Both Debbi Steele and the young woman were winners, and Debbi didn't have to work late to catch up.

I often get thirty calls a month from people who want to take me to lunch so they can ask me questions about how to become a speaker. I reply, "No, I can't have lunch with you, but I'll give you five minutes. If we were at lunch, what would you ask me?" Nine out of ten can't think of a question! There are so many terrific books out there full of the "secrets," so, if you plan to pick the brains of successful people, do your own research first so you can make the most of your time and theirs. (If you're interested in speaking, read *Speaking Secrets of the Masters*, one of the books I've co-authored. Ordering information is in the back of this book.)

Things to Think About Before Saying "Yes"

- Do I really want to do what I've been asked to do?

- Will I benefit personally from the experience?

- Will those closest to me benefit?

- Will I ever have the opportunity to do this again?

- How much of my time is involved?

- Can the job be done quickly, or will it involve weeks, months, or a year?

- How much help will I have, or do I have full responsibility?

- Am I being asked to do this job because I'm right for it or because I usually don't say "no"?

- Will my family or friends have to take a back seat while I'm involved?

- Will I have to cancel other plans to make this new commitment?

- Does it sound fun?

- Does it sound challenging?

- Will I need to learn a new skill?

If you don't have the right answers to these questions, teach yourself to say "no." Or to say "yes" by saying "no" and then offering an alternative.

Make Meetings Work for You

Meetings are one of the biggest time wasters in business. Nobody benefits from poorly run meetings. Schedule your meetings in a cluster. If they are stretched out through the day or week, you will do little but mark time between them. Having them scheduled back-to-back with brief time buffers between motivates others to use you well during your time with them. It also sets a deadline and gets you out of those endless tail-chasing or finger-pointing sessions that pass for communication in some organizations.

- Start on time. The moment people assume meetings will start late, they'll gradually show up later and later.

- Have an agenda with a set time frame. If the meeting will be short, *stand up!* Don't let people get comfortable.

- Reinforce time limits by scheduling meetings at the end of the day or before lunch when people want to leave.

- Call on experts. Learn to use the intelligence and knowledge of other people. Only fools pretend they already know everything.

- Substitute on-line meetings if possible.

Don't Be Perfect *All* the Time

Murray Raphel is a direct-mail specialist in Atlantic City as well as a best-selling author. He is a gold mine of information and shares it very generously. Whenever he is contacted for an idea or opinion, he immediately turns to his keyboard and hunts and pecks a reply. In the days before word processors, someone once called him to criticize his spelling and typing. Murray asked, "Did you understand what the note said?"

"Yes," the complainer replied.

"How long do you plan to keep my note?" Murray asked.

"I've already done what you suggested and thrown it away," the man replied. Even with today's electronic media, I suspect he doesn't bother running a spell check on such messages, but his information is still excellent and quick. Murray's point: "Some things have to be done perfectly. Some things don't." Avoid striving for perfection in things that don't matter. People are usually paid to get results, not to be perfect.

And don't waste your time on regrets. Trying to rewrite history is futile. Don't spend precious minutes rehashing former decisions, justifying bad ones, or salvaging poor time investments that ought to be written off. Use the past as a guide for the future, not as an excuse for not dealing with it.

Do It Now

Don't procrastinate. One of the biggest reasons people are unsuccessful is they wait to do something until it doesn't matter any more—in which case, they've lost more than just time. They have surrendered control of their lives to others or to random chance.

Indecision is often a form of procrastination. There is a time for deliberation and a time for action. The well-known prayer might be altered to "Lord, give me the patience to wait for the right moment, the energy to act decisively, and the wisdom to know when to do which."

Take Control of the Telephone

We can't live with them and we can't live without them. Telephones are the indispensable monsters of modern society. Take charge of your phone.

- Devise a way to get off before you get on. Say things like, "I just have two minutes; this is why I called."

- Don't automatically ask, "How are you?" People will either automatically reply "fine" or, if they've just gotten divorced, fallen in love, or been ill, take twenty minutes of your day to tell you how they really are. Express your personal interest in people in other ways. When you open every phone conversation with several minutes of social positioning, you stand a good chance of not getting to the point of your call before your listener is summoned away.

- When someone asks me, "How are you?" and I know it's just a preprogrammed conversation opener, I usually answer, "Busy. Tell me, what can I do for you?" If they say, "Can I ask you a question?" I reply, "You can ask me two as long as

I can answer them in two minutes." Both answers indicate a genuine concern in the other person's business, but free me of time-wasting preparatory chat. In business, efficiency can be better manners than insincere, ritualistic exchanges.

- Before you pick up the phone to call someone, make a written outline of the topics you want to discuss. This will save calling back.

- If your business requires you to call people, make your telephone calls early in the morning. The people you're calling are more likely to be in their offices then and at their best. People often get irritated as the day goes on. If you're in a job where you are soliciting appointments or business by telephone, it is especially important to call people early, before they get bogged down.

- If you have trouble ending a long-winded, one-sided conversation, try one of these, said very cheerfully:
  "Well, I won't keep you..."
  "Oh, there's my other line..."
  "Oops, the doorbell! We'll talk more later..."

- If you leave a message on someone's voice mail, be very upbeat, very specific, describe the information you need so people can leave the answer on your voice mail or answering machine. Be sure to give your name and number!

- Update your own voice mail or answering machine message whenever you will be away from your phone. One of my pet peeves is having no idea when people are going to get my message. We change the outgoing message on our office machine every time we go out: "Going to lunch"—"Closed for the day"— "Patricia will be back at two o'clock." That way people know when to expect a response.

- Leave your web site address so anyone who needs immediate information can get it.

Use E-mail Effectively

"The first time I tried e-mail," I used to joke, "I almost electrocuted myself licking the stamp." Today I couldn't be without it.

A lot of people think e-mail has depersonalized relationships, but that's not true. It is nearly as immediate as a phone call, but more polite because it allows the recipient to respond at his or her convenience. So many businesspeople are rarely at their desks that e-mail can be the best way to communicate, saving days of phone tag. I tell other speakers, "Don't call and ask me for advice. I'm not here, or if I am, I'm busy. But if you e-mail me, I can respond on my own time, on a plane, late at night, or while I watch the news." Also, with my electronic *Speaker Fripp News*, I can communicate with a lot of people all at once, and it costs nothing to send it. E-mail is a valuable tool for guarding your money, your time, and your energy, and, at the same time, lets you be responsive to a large number of people.

Some Time-Savers at Work

- Go to work before or after the rush hours. Beat the traffic.

- When you go to a parking garage, don't drive around the lower levels searching for a spot; drive straight to the top, where you know you can park.

- In small buildings, don't wait for elevators; walk.

- Take a meditation break rather than a coffee break.

- Handle paperwork only once. Every time you pick up a piece of paper, rip off the corner. If you pick it up a second time and you haven't finished with it, rip another corner. If you pick it up again and still don't do anything with it, rip another corner. This way, if you keep picking it up, eventually your problem is eliminated.

- Keep all your important papers, notes, and plans in one place.

- Get somebody else to scan magazines and rip out articles that may be of interest to you, or do so yourself and read them on an airplane or while waiting for appointments. Consider subscribing to a clipping service if you want to keep on top of a special field. Use a calendar system that works for you. In her book, *How to Put More Life in Your Time*, Dru Scott Decker suggests you buy yourself a handsome leather folder with your name embossed on it—something so beautiful you won't lose it.

- Confirm, don't assume. Planes get canceled, people forget, messages get garbled, important papers slip behind filing cabinets. Save yourself hours by taking a minute to confirm. Don't assume, because you made an appointment with someone, that person is going to be there. Confirm before you leave. Don't assume the plane is on time. Call the airport. Don't assume that everyone will know exactly what to do for an important event. Confirm, confirm, confirm.

- Learn from other people's experience. Don't reinvent the wheel. Consult people, books, and organizations that can help you.

- Learn to do research on your computer.

- Do several things at once when it's appropriate. Listen to informational tapes while you're driving a car or riding on an airplane. Have a headset on your telephone so you can write checks and open mail while being kept on hold. At home, exercise and watch TV at the same time.

Handling Mail

- When you're sorting your mail, put your fun mail (notes from friends) aside to open when you have time to sit with your feet up.

- Learn to sift rapidly through junk mail for the few items of interest. (But be careful—credit cards are often sent in boring envelopes to confuse thieves.)

- Answer mail by recycling letters. It's quite acceptable to write notations on the letters you receive and send them back or fax the reply. Make a photocopy if you want one for your file.

Handling People

- Always go to the office of the person you want to talk to. It's a lot easier to get out of somebody else's office than to push them out of yours. And don't allow long-winded visitors to sit in your office. Keep them standing.

- Whenever you plan to meet someone, especially someone in the habit of arriving late, be sure to meet him or her in a place where you can accomplish something while you're waiting.

- If a salesperson wants to talk to you, say, "I'll give you twenty minutes if you want to come and talk to me while I eat my lunch." (This worked for me when I had a salon, although it's not so appropriate now.) When you agree to hear a sales presentation, you have a right to limit the time.

Managing at Home

- Make blender meals when you're alone. Protein powder, fruit, and milk or fruit juice mixed in a blender is very filling, very nutritious, and very quick.

- Eat out. This especially saves time in restaurants you visit frequently (unless you use dinner out as a time to relax). Then you don't even have to look at the menu. When your food is brought to you, ask for the check.

- If you can, pay other people to do things for you—to shop, clean your house, garden, or make repairs.

- Make sure you have a spare of any appliance you use frequently. Then, if one of them breaks, you don't go crazy.

- Do your shopping by phone or computer.

- Buy in quantity. My father's philosophy was "if you want ten, buy a hundred wholesale." As a time management technique, I buy thirty birthday cards at a time and ten tubes of toothpaste. It cuts down shopping time.

Personal Time-Savers

- Meet with your friends in groups rather than individually to keep up with friendships when your time is short. Breakfast is good.

- Make appointments with yourself. For me, it's important to spend at least fifteen minutes soaking in a bubble-bath now and then. (I think this comforting diversion should be on everyone's schedule, for his or her peace of mind.)

- For women: Consider wearing your hair short, unless you're prepared to invest a lot of time in maintaining it long. Or wear it long enough to twist up with pins, avoiding time with hot rollers and styling brushes.

- Have a wardrobe consultant or someone else whose taste you trust preview clothes for you. This way you go straight to the store and try on the possibles instead of spending hours or days sifting through racks. (Not to be confused with shopping as recreation which is fine once in a while.)

- Learn how to cope with unwanted invitations. Never feel bad for refusing. Try saying, "Thank you. I appreciate the invitation, but I've already made plans." You don't have to explain that your plan is to stay home with your feet up and read a trashy thriller or go to a movie by yourself or catch up on your e-mail. The *San Francisco Chronicle* once published an article about how people decline invitations. One woman interviewed said, "Thank you, but my husband hates social gatherings." Businesswoman Ellen Newman favored more tactful honesty. If it's a free night, she tells people she and her husband "need that time very badly for ourselves." Playwright Anita Loos wished she had the integrity to respond the way a friend of hers did. He wrote, "Mr. John Golden sincerely regrets he has no desire to accept your kind invitation."

- Minimize lunch dates. They break up the day. I do have dinner with friends, but rarely lunch. If someone insists on a midday get-together "to treat you to lunch," I suggest we talk while walking in Golden Gate Park, a block from my house. I can always squeeze in another walk, but I can't squeeze in another meal. Also, as a home-based businessperson, I dress casually when I'm not on the road. To go out to lunch, I have to dress up and make up, drive downtown, have lunch, drive back. Not a big treat!

- Start your Christmas shopping in January. Once a month, write all your birthday cards and put Post-its® on with what day you need to post them, or jot "mail Sam's birthday card" on your calendar. Have a dozen clever gifts tucked away that are appropriate for anybody.

Know when you are your best and most energetic. For most people, that's in the morning. Plan to be doing the most important things when you're in top form. Try to eliminate one time waster from your life each week.

Balancing on the High Wire

Nancy Austin wrote *A Passion for Excellence* with Tom Peters and *The Assertive Woman* with Stanlee Phelps. She's always being asked business questions, but in predominantly female groups, women frequently ask a question she never hears from men. These women are just starting a new business or a new job. "I don't want to surrender my life to it," they say, "so how can I balance everything I have to do?"

Suddenly every eye is fixed on Nancy. "From my perch up there on the stage," Nancy told me, "I watch with growing alarm as a room full of women get ready to download every smidgen of my winning strategy for success—if only I had one! I have to tell them there is no tidy formula and no such thing as real balance, only a series of cruel and grinding choices."

Charles Garfield, author of *Peak Performers: The New Heroes of American Business*, told me the same thing over lunch one day. "Peak performers," he said, "don't usually have balance on a daily basis."

Have I had it all? No, but I've had everything I wanted. You ask, "So you have a great life, but what's the message for me?" Here's my message: Turn your disadvantages into advantages. Always turn up. Develop excellent work habits. And accept temporary imbalance while striving for balance over the long haul.

Three Coping Styles

Life has never been simple, and each generation is always sure the decisions and choices they face each day are harder than ever before in history. We do have many more options, but instead of making things easier, this multiplicity of choices can be stressful, even immobilizing. It's like facing the world's biggest smorgasbord table and not knowing where to start.

There are three basic ways of dealing with the multiple demands of our personal lives, job, home, and community.

1. *Limiting.* Avoid conflicts by focusing totally on one area, usually career. Efficient but restrictive.

2. *Staggering.* Devote time blocks alternately to different demands. "This year I'll concentrate on making vice president, next year I'll get my body in shape, the year after that I'll go back to school and maybe get married."

3. *Juggling.* Participate in all important areas at once, juggling the time and energy demands on an as-needed basis.

Juggling has some distinct benefits. You get to try all the goodies on the table at once. But juggling is also the most difficult. Jugglers need strong support systems, both within their families and in the community.

According to Dr. Rela Geffen Monson, who conducted a study of one thousand high-level professional and career women, American women have a strong tendency to cope by limiting—avoiding conflict with careers by not marrying, or by marrying but not having children. Interestingly, however, two-thirds of the Jewish women who took part in the study were married, and most had children. "The majority of [these] respondents saw some positive connection between their commitment to...the Jewish community and their professional lives." Apparently these women juggled rather than resorting to limiting or staggering because their work gave them a vital sense of connectedness to their community. If your work has the same kind of meaning to you, you are more likely to wind up a juggler.

How you choose to cope is a matter of personal style, personal resources, and what you are up against.

YOUR ASSIGNMENT:
Budgeting Your Time

FRIPPICISM

Learn to say "no" without feeling guilty. Learn also to offer an alternative that is better for you.

---

1. What would I do with an extra hour in each day?

2. How much time did I spend today working on my A goals?

3. What do I want to eliminate from my life?

4. Can I do it?

5. What are my biggest time wasters?

6. Would getting up an hour earlier be practical?

7. Would getting up an hour earlier be profitable?

8. When can I schedule an hour of uninterrupted time for one of my A projects?

9. What telephoning strategies would work best for me?

10. How can I make my To-Do lists more effective?

11. What would make my work environment more efficient?

12. Do I need to schedule more time for self-improvement? If so, when? In what areas?

13. Do I need to schedule more time to exercise? If so, when?

14. Do I need to schedule more time for the special people in my life? If so, when?

15. What will I say, the next time I want to say "no"?

16. How can I use my travel and waiting time more productively?

17. What jobs and responsibilities can I delegate?

18. The next time someone asks me to do something they probably could and should do for themselves, what will I say?

19. What will I do to make my next meeting more efficient?

20. How will I eliminate unnecessary paperwork?

21. What strategies will I try out to control unwelcome interruptions and drop-in visitors rather than allowing them to control me?

22. What one time waster will I eliminate this week?

Homework Assignment

The next time you say "no" successfully, give yourself a special treat.

CHAPTER 13

Seven Tips for Turning Potential into Performance

FRIPPICISM
You have to master technique so you can abandon it.
Robert Fripp

Here are ten tips for turning your potential into positive actions. At the end of this chapter, you'll have a chance to consider the best way to use these tips to keep yourself moving forward.

1. Understand which things deserve your energy

With so many fascinating opportunities before you each day, how do you decide which are for you? My brother, Robert, has formulated four questions for judging whether an action is appropriate for him.

- *Does this earn a living for me?* In a material world, we all have responsibilities that cannot be ignored.

- *Can I learn from this?* Can I grow as a human being by doing this particular piece of work?

- *Can I have fun?* If I can't have fun doing whatever I'm doing, if I can't enjoy it, then it's really not worth doing; if life is only drudgery, it's hardly worth living.

- *Is it useful?* Sooner or later any piece of useful work will involve us with other people. Will this action bring me together with people in a worthwhile way?

These are Robert Fripp's four criteria. My brother explains, "When I confront something, these are the things I use to measure my chances for a positive outcome."

2. Recognize the difference between "low-payoff" and "high-payoff" activities

When you invest your time, you want to invest it in high-return projects. The lists below provide a profile of the activities with the potential for the highest return.

Characteristics of low-payoff activities	Characteristics of high-payoff activities
Not related to goal	Directly related to goal
Comfortable to do	Might not be pleasant
No risk involved	Tend to involve risk
Routine	Might be difficult
Trivial	Important
Noncreative, anyone can do it	Can't be delegated

Investing your time and energy is like investing your money. You may risk it and lose it. But risk is what spells the difference between getting what you want and sitting on the sidelines.

3. Resist emotional blackmail

A woman at a seminar asked what she should do when she's going to work in the evening and her two-year-old says, "Mommy, I hate you because you're going out." I turned to the audience for answers. One woman stood up and said, "You are allowing yourself to be emotionally blackmailed." Another woman said, "I get the same thing, and I smile and hug her and say, 'I'm going to miss you too, honey. I'll be back as soon as I can.' It's up to you whether you interpret your child's fears as blackmail or not."

Another woman came up to me at the break because she did not want to share her thoughts with the group. She said, "If I can make my mentally retarded two-year-old daughter understand that Mommy is going out to make money to help buy her 'pretties,' I think somebody should certainly be able to make a normal child understand."

Blackmail is a contract between two people. It only works when both agree to play. We should not accept emotional blackmail from others, just as we should not try to blackmail them. My wonderful friend, Karen Trunnelle Dyer, who spent countless hours typing the first edition of this book in the days before word processors, had small children who would sometimes make noise and demand her attention when she was hard at work. She would explain to them, "I am doing this to make more money for all of us. You can help me by playing peacefully near me, but not interrupting."

"They learned," Karen told me, "that kisses and catastrophes are more important than money and I could always be interrupted for them, but pointless interruptions resulted in fewer treats. When children feel they are contributing by cooperating and sharing in the results, they are more willing to keep the interruptions to a minimum."

Often society provides women with only a vague line between good manners and being taken advantage of, between being a caring, nurturing person and being a victim. It's up to the woman to make the line clear and strong, both for herself and for others. Joann, the wife of a speaker friend, was formerly married to a man who treated her shabbily. Finally, she thought to herself: "If I were being treated this way by a man courting me, I wouldn't dream of marrying him." In a matter of days, she had filed for divorce and has never regretted that decision.

To teach people how we want them to treat us, we must sometimes use a little muscle and refuse to be intimidated. We need to know we deserve good treatment. If we don't respect ourselves, who will?

4. Begin to think about your retirement now

Recently, I went to the memorial service of my friend Milt Eisele, a famous wine-grape grower in Napa, California, and one of the nicest and best-loved people I've known. The event was a very happy and upbeat celebration of a remarkable life. Milt is a perfect example of someone who lived every day of his life. He was married to his wife Barbara for fifty-six years, and every day, for fifty-six years, when she prepared him a meal, he thanked her for it. A wonderful man.

Years ago, Milt told me a story that made a lasting impression. "When I was around forty-six or so," he said, "I had a remarkable experience. I was invited to go to lunch with employees in the Sears, Roebuck home office. They were retiring one of their old telephone operators. My host told me about Sears' experiment with counseling their retirees. Ten years prior to your actual retirement, the personnel department called you in. Everyone would shake hands with you and say, 'Ten years from today, we're going to do this for keeps. Now what are you going to do when you retire?' The typical answer was, 'Well, I'm going to go fishing' or 'go hunting.' 'I'm going to travel,' or 'I'm going to play golf.'

"So Sears arranged to have people prepare for these objectives during this ten-year period. This process made most of them realize that just golf or travel wouldn't fulfill them—and they came to this realization when they still had ten years to plan."

Milt had another cautionary story. About eight years later, a neighbor of his retired. The man had been president of one of the largest railroads in the country, but now the company had dropped him from their board. Like many retired executives, he and his wife went to Europe, bought a Mercedes, and toured for six months. When he came home, he suddenly thought, "What in the world will I do with myself?"

"Since we lived near Stanford University," Milt told me, "it seemed appropriate that Stanford would have him lecture at their Business School or in their Department of Economics or Finance. But they didn't. I would see him frequently, particularly on Sunday mornings while I was working in my garden, and we would chat.

"Then he was gone for about three months. I thought he was away traveling or on a cruise.

"One Saturday morning he reappeared. I was startled at his appearance. He had two or three days' growth of beard, his pants were not pressed, and he was wearing bedroom slippers. I was really taken aback. 'My God,' I muttered, 'What's happened to you?'

"'Well, I really wasn't feeling very well,' he explained, 'so they put me in the hospital for a couple of months. They couldn't find anything wrong with me, but I continued to feel lousy and they decided the best thing for me was to return home and be with my wife and friends. You know,' he said after a minute, 'I still feel lousy.'

"Eighteen months later he was dead.

"I don't think he lasted more than five years after his retirement. This said to me that you've got to have some challenges, some feeling of achievement each day. If not, before long, you won't be looking at just the end of the day."

5. Make contracts with yourself—before someone else makes them for you

A psychiatrist wrote about a woman who wanted to give up smoking but couldn't. He asked her, "Do you really want to?" She said, "Yes." "Okay," he said, "anytime you smoke, you have to give me ten dollars which I'll donate to the cause of my choice. I know you're active in Mothers Against Drunk Drivers, so I'll use the money to sponsor beer-guzzling contests at local colleges and send MADD regular updated notices of how much beer you're buying."

Moral: It's better to write your own contracts.

6. Look behind you

A friend I made through running was David Leof, a psychiatrist. One day we jogged from the Marina Green to the Golden Gate Bridge and back again. Afterward, we were walking to cool down. The sky was clear and full of seagulls, the water was blue and full of boats, and the bridge arched over the entrance to the harbor. As we turned back toward our car, we saw the greenery and the trees of the Marina Green, joggers stretching, and rows of neat Spanish-style houses.

David said, "You see what we've just done, Patricia? We have just turned around a few degrees, and it's like we're looking at two totally different cities. The good thing about my practice is that people only have to change their thinking a few degrees to have totally different lives."

We've all heard people say, "Well, it's not working where I am. I think I'm going to move to another state, divorce my spouse, sell my children, go into a different line of business, lose fifty pounds, or bleach my hair blonde, and then my life will work." When it comes to good mental health, sometimes we just have to realize what we already have to be grateful for, just change our thinking a few degrees. The next time you feel stale or frustrated, look at where you are and what you have from a slightly different angle.

7. Start the day right

How you start out in the morning sets the tone for how the rest of the day will go. If you're an "owl" instead of a "lark," the morning is no time for reality. It's too easy to feel pressured as you rush to get ready. You end up nagging others (or yourself) about all the things they forgot to do yesterday and must remember to do today. That's one reason why lists made the night before are invaluable.

Be sure you create a positive atmosphere at home with affirmations of love and support for your dear ones. Continue your positive pattern with everyone you meet. I used to park at a large downtown garage at six o'clock in the morning. When I got there, the nice young men would say, "How are you, Miss Fripp?" I'd say, "Terrific! Marvelous! Great! Never felt so good in all my life." Obviously, that wasn't always true. But people react to you the way you present yourself to them, and you react to their reaction.

After I had parked there for a couple of years, one of the young attendants confided, "Miss Fripp, you are the only regular we dare ask, 'How are you?' We have a game to see who gets to you first." My cheerful morning greeting, intended to raise my own spirits, had paid other dividends. Some of those nice young men even came to me for haircuts. And don't you think they may have put themselves out to extricate my car in the afternoon crush, for that nice Miss Fripp who always acted so pleased to see them rather than some miserable old crab who came there early in the morning? There are so many people who help your life go smoothly who are not on your payroll.

If it's biologically possible, get an early start. I know there are morning people and night people, but you know who got the worm. Most people are at their best and most positive in the morning, so take advantage of that positivity by being there to work with them. Get up as early as possible (what I call "rolling out of bed on the right side"). If you want to start getting up an hour earlier than you have been, don't do it all of a sudden.

Work up to it. Start getting up ten or fifteen minutes earlier for a week, then another ten or fifteen minutes earlier the next.

Reward yourself for getting to work early. (I have my first cup of coffee, then go to the gym.) Promise yourself that if you get up an hour earlier and accomplish such-and-such by ten o'clock, you will allow yourself to put your feet up for ten minutes, read a marvelous, informative book (like this one), and have a healthful snack. Program rewards into your schedule, and also punishments for when you indulge in unproductive behaviors. For example, if you say "yes" to somebody when you want to say "no," penalize yourself by balancing your checkbook without a calculator.

YOUR ASSIGNMENT:
Turning Potential into Performance

FRIPPICISM

Thank everyone. (I am usually the only person who thanks the drivers on the long-term parking shuttle buses.)

For the following tips, see where you stand and where you'd like to go.

Understand which things deserve your energy.

Some things I want to give more attention are:

Some things I want to give less attention are:

Know the difference between low-payoff and high-payoff activities.

My high-payoff activities are:

My low-payoff activities are:

Which of these low-payoff activities can I discard?

Resist emotional blackmail.

Someone who can usually get me to do something I don't want to do is:

The emotional blackmail used is:

I agree to this blackmail because I:

Next time, my response will be:

Make contracts with yourself—before someone else makes them for you.

A contract I want to make is:

A contract I *need* to make is:

Start the day right.

My mornings
☐ are great.
☐ could be better.
☐ are a disaster.

To make them (even) better, I will:

CHAPTER 14

Possibilities

> ### FRIPPICISM
>
> *In life, no one is dealt all the aces.*
> *You just have to play the hand you*
> *have better than other people.*
>
> ARTHUR HENRY FRIPP

Your whole life is a shifting prism of opportunities—your possibilities. No matter how much energy, persistence, and confidence you focus on your goals, you will miss some of the good stuff if you fail to notice opportunity. Keep yourself constantly open to possibilities.

Possibilities to do *what*? Whatever it is you dream of. When I was twelve years old, I didn't know what was going to happen to me, but I promised myself two things. First, I was going to be glamorous. Second, I would have an exciting life. To me that meant getting off airplanes with a mink coat over my shoulder, just like the movie stars. I have a vivid picture of sitting in my father's office and seeing a picture in a magazine of a movie star in gorgeous clothes getting off an airplane. Although I had no idea how, I had a vivid picture of wearing those clothes and flying in those planes.

A few years ago, I was speaking to a large group in Hawaii. I commented it had never occurred to me when I was just starting out that one day I'd have the life I have now.

Afterwards, my friend Don Thoren came up to me. "Patricia, that isn't true," he said. "I heard you tell my son at dinner last night about that magazine picture. You always knew what you were going to do, you just didn't know how you were going to do it." It's true. While my friends wanted to marry millionaires, I knew I'd rather be one.

At age fifteen, I started an apprenticeship to become a hairdresser. You may think that's a long way from fame, fortune, glamour, and travel; yet since I have passed the age of fifty, my friends tease me that I have created my own version of "Lifestyles of the Rich and Famous." I travel seventy percent of my life, frequently to fabulous places like Bermuda, Hawaii, the Bahamas, Orlando, and Las Vegas, addressing audiences as large as 10,000 for Fortune 500 companies. I was the first woman president of the National Speakers Association, founding president of the largest NSA chapter in northern California, and I am the only person in the NSA who has earned every award and designation given, the Certified Speaking Professional (CSP) for experience, the Cavett for contributions to the speaking profession, and the Council of Peers Award of Excellence, the highest award given for excellence on the speaking platform. There are others who've gotten all the awards and been president, but I'm the only one who's *also* been president of his or her local chapter. In my world, that's pretty big stuff.

I'm not telling you this to impress you with my importance or achievements. It's to impress you with the possibilities you can create in your life and all around you. Remember Woody Allen's comment that "eighty percent of life is just turning up." To me that means going out and participating in the world. You don't get discovered if you stay home. You don't fall in love without sometimes smiling at a stranger. You don't write a masterpiece until you sit down and pick up your pen. You don't become a great speaker until you have practiced before dozens and dozens of Rotary Clubs. You don't run a marathon until you call one of your pals and say, "Hey, let's go out for a brisk walk." Possibilities.

Make Yourself Indispensable

After eight years of running the office for her husband, speaker Scott McKain, Sheri McKain got a different job as an $18,000-a-year secretary, working for a friend in a licensing company. She had no job description. In fact, many people thought Sheri was the nanny because whenever her boss, who had a new baby, was on the phone and the baby cried, Sheri would whisk it out of the room.

Sheri didn't see herself as a flunky. She took the initiative, reading the files, talking to customers, and attending trade shows. Soon she knew more about the profession than almost anyone else. Through her direct efforts, business increased five times. In just four years, her income grew from $18,000 to the top one percent of all women in the United States. Currently, her responsibilities include licensing the works of the well-loved artist Norman Rockwell.

Someone without a job title made herself indispensable.

"That's Impossible"

When Ted Turner decided to start an all-news television network, he was assured it would be a flop. The existing networks were losing money on their news programs and only continued them as a public service. But Turner persisted. He started CNN, now a major international force in news gathering and broadcasting.

Did you know that Debbi Fields' friends told her it was a dumb idea to open a cookie store? She said, "Maybe it is, but I won't be satisfied unless I try." She was a nervous wreck when she started her business, Mrs. Fields' Cookies.

Did you know that an ABC executive once said to Barbara Walters, "You'll never make it in broadcasting. Your energy level is wrong, and you've got a speech impediment"?

Did you know that a Hollywood director told Burt Reynolds he couldn't act and told Clint Eastwood his Adam's apple was too big? As they were walking down the street afterward, Reynolds commented to Eastwood, "Well, I can learn to act, but what are you going to do?"

Decca Records told the young Beatles there was no market for singing groups with guitars, but they persisted. My brother once refused to hire Elton John, saying his singing wasn't good enough, but Elton persisted. Josephine Baker was told she was too distinctive to dance in the chorus, so she became a star instead. Jay Leno was told he'd never make it in showbusiness unless he had plastic surgery because his face, according to one agent, "would scare off children." Director after director told Danny DeVito he was too short to be cast as anything but a freak. Then there's business student Fred Smith whose idea for a corporation got low marks from his professor, but who went ahead and founded Federal Express anyway. Basketball legend Michael Jordan was cut from his high school basketball team, and Reggie Miller's parents were told he might never walk properly, but he became the second best shooting guard in the NBA.

The moral is that only *you* should decide what's impossible and what isn't.

"Everything I Do Is Exciting"

Once upon a time, I addressed a crowd of 3,000 with none other than Dr. Norman Vincent Peale. He was then eighty-six years old and had more vitality and energy than you and I put together. Sharing a limousine with him afterwards, I used the opportunity to ask him, "What's the most exciting thing in your life?"

He thought for a moment and mentioned traveling and his farm. "Well, actually, Patricia," he said, "everything I do I find exciting." This proves there is possibility for joy and excitement in your life well into your eighties. But obviously you have to be doing something before you can get excited about doing it.

My Most Unforgettable Character

Tricia Defibaugh has a true rags-to-riches story. Today Tricia is chairman of the board of Aloette Cosmetics, a big transition for a woman who got married in traditional times, determined to be a good wife, have a couple of kids, and live happily ever after. Her husband decided her dream was not his dream. Tricia found herself with a three-year-old daughter and a broken marriage.

In the midst of the emotional shock of the divorce, Tricia realized she had to find work, even though she had never had any desire to be a businesswoman and doubted her ability to support herself adequately. Because of her conservative Mennonite background, she was not used to the idea of women working, and she felt guilty about leaving her young daughter.

Financial need forced her to take in a boarder. Her first job was as a part-time receptionist in a beauty salon at minimum wage. Then, in exploring other part-time employment opportunities, she learned about the home-show cosmetics business. Since most of the sales demonstrations were scheduled for evenings, she could be at home with her daughter during the day and make full-time earnings by working part-time hours several evenings a week. Within one year, she was promoted to vice president of that company, and her career in beauty and sales was firmly established.

She met her present husband, John, who not only believed in her, but encouraged her to enter direct sales. Tricia and John eventually started Aloette Cosmetics.

Today Aloette is a leading force in cosmetics direct sales, both in the United States and abroad. In 1996, its nineteenth year of business, Aloette had 82 outlets in seven countries and sales of $11.6 million.

Tricia is the force behind Aloette's sales and marketing department. Aloette, based in Malvern, Pennsylvania, went public in 1986 and was cited by *Inc. Magazine* as one of America's fastest-growing privately held corporations for the two consecutive years prior to the public offering.

Tricia's and John's success did not just happen like magic. It has taken more than twenty years of persistence and determination, discipline, and enthusiasm to make Aloette the company it now is, but it all began because Tricia made herself aware of the possibilities available to her. Tricia has discovered something she is very good at, made a science of it, and taught others how to do the same things she does.

Tricia's story, from her traditional and conservative upbringing through her personal growth to the person she has become today, is a classic story of triumphing over adversity. It is a story of possibilities.

My Second Most Unforgettable Character

Actually there is a second person I will never forget, a man who had lost a million dollars by the time he was twenty-five years old. The story is not how John McCormack lost it, but how he made it back.

When I met him, John was in the hairstyling business. Now, as you well know by now, I had been in the same business and made a pretty good living at it, but I could not believe what this guy had done. He and his wife had eighteen salons, with more than $15 million in sales the year before. I was fascinated and had to learn his story.

John McCormack was not a hairdresser himself, but his wife was. Years before, in his single days, he had been a New York City policeman. He did a couple of entrepreneurial things like buying some Christmas trees and reselling them. But he realized that, although he loved being a policeman, he had to do something else if he wanted any real economic stability.

John became a stockbroker. Times were good, and he invested in some small companies that were doing well. At age twenty-five, he was worth a million dollars on paper. Then the economy changed, and all the little companies he held stock in went out of business. His own company folded, and he was unemployed. John felt burned out, useless, lethargic. His girlfriend, Maryanne, dumped him. Then she took him back.

Each morning he would drive her to work, and then he would go to stare at the ocean.

So, at twenty-seven, John was walking down the beach one day, flat broke and really down. He met an old man who said, "Hey, young fellow, why are you so depressed?"

He replied, "I just lost a million dollars."

The old man said, "How old are you?"

"Twenty-seven."

"Well, congratulations! It took me till I was forty to lose my first million!" the old man said.

John returned to the beach every day over the next three weeks, and each time he stopped to talk with the man he calls Abe. Abe told John he had lost everything he owned on three different occasions and learned something new each time.

John began to regain his confidence. "He had me list all my assets: I could speak English, I had a lot of friends, I liked numbers, and I could find my way around. It was not the greatest balance sheet, but it was more than a lot of people have." Abe urged John to go to work for somebody who had started with even less than that.

John got a job with a firm that sold industrial washing machines. His boss, Bernie Milch, was Polish, a survivor of a World War II concentration camp. When they first talked about the business, John was skeptical about selling washing machines and started to leave. Milch called after him, "I made $13 million last year selling washing machines." That got John's attention. John learned everything about production and sales from Milch, and, in return, he provided some financial expertise Milch's company didn't have. While John was out selling washing machines, he met an Italian immigrant named Nick Leone.

Nick Leone had been a chef before he came by freighter to America. When the freighter docked in Philadelphia, he jumped ship. Speaking no English, he first got a job as a janitor and then as a chef. He worked hard until he was able to open his own catering business on Long Island.

Leone charged eight dollars a person for banquets, and he was doing okay. Then he hired an architect to draw up plans for a beautiful banquet facility, the kind of place where people could hold large parties and gladly pay twenty dollars or more per person. Using the sketches and his vision of a greatly expanded business, Leone persuaded some of his suppliers to advance him credit. With his cash freed up, Leone built the hall. It was so successful he soon was able to build a second one. Leone's "Italian math" inspired John: "He wasn't just a chef and he wasn't just a manager. He was a creator." John and Leone struck up a friendship that eventually turned into a business partnership. They are still in business together and have a lot of different projects.

Then John and Maryanne got married. She was running a successful hair salon in Valley Stream, New York. She convinced John that precision haircutting was the coming trend in the haircutting industry. They decided to establish an innovative chain of upscale, high-volume hair salons.

A common theory is businesses fail because they do not have enough resources, but John believes many failures occur because businesses don't set their sights high enough. John and Maryanne weren't opening just any hairstyling salon, so they didn't open it in just any place. Because of his travels as a business consultant, John had decided Texas was the place to start. The salons would be fashionable, located in strategic shopping malls, and appeal to both men and women. The staff would be well trained in a precision haircutting technique developed by Maryanne and would be dedicated to customer service. In early 1976, John and Maryanne opened Visible Changes in Houston, Texas.

John worked for three years to develop an extensive professional business plan. Even though he and Maryanne had sufficient capital to start the business, they had to make presentations to over three hundred banks before getting additional financing.

The success of Visible Changes launched a number of mega-chain rivals. However, Visible Changes employees can make substantial wages and have pension plans, unlike other operations that have poorly paid and exploited stylists who offer erratic service. Hairstyling is too often a high-turnover, dead-end job with little loyalty between employer and employee. According to Bruce G. Posner and Bob Burlingham in their *Inc. Magazine* profile of John McCormack, eighty percent of the haircuts done in America today are still done by businesses with only one salon. But that is changing, and John's vision is one of the reasons. He believes the future of hairstyling lies with highly trained, highly motivated professionals who can advance within their company.

John and Maryanne interviewed nearly three hundred hair cutters for their first salon. Finally they found five hair cutters and a manager willing to risk the new approach. The first employees worked twelve-hour days for just fifteen dollars because they believed in John's and Maryanne's dream. They knew they would share whatever success followed.

The first Houston salon offered free haircuts during its first six weeks of operations. Visible Changes, John explained, was introducing a revolutionary new haircutting system, and they did not want their customers to pay for it until it was perfected. The salon was a huge success.

When John and Maryanne started Visible Changes, the corporate headquarters was in their home. In 1979, they moved into an actual office space, and in 1981, they became one of the first companies in the industry to be fully computerized. John can tell you the previous day's income at each location and compare it to the other days, weeks, or months. He can show exactly how much business each employee has done, the age and sex of the customer mix at each location, which customers are coming back, and each individual customer's birthday, anniversary, children's ages, date of last visit, and number of visits this year.

Working with his employees, John has evolved a system of commissions and bonuses that lets motivated employees earn several times more in income and benefits than they could make anywhere else. The average employee earns triple the industry average, and some make more than twice that much. Customers also get better service than they could get almost anywhere else. Each new hairstylist must achieve rigorous standards within six months. If they don't, they're not Visible Changes caliber and they're out.

Company sales grew from $1.3 million in 1979 to $35 million in 1996. Innovative marketing techniques have kept Visible Changes growing during recessions. To create a broader economic base, John set up a company to package and sell his unique computer program to other salons. He also became a partner in a business to produce and market a line of hair products sold only through salons. The hair products did $2 million of business in their first eight months. The computer programs sold $1 million worth in ten months.

Twenty years later, Visible Changes has seventeen salons. John is CEO, and Maryanne is President. To celebrate their anniversary, they rewarded their top-producing stylists with a vacation in Australia. John is still great pals with Nick Leone, his old partner in the catering business. And his 1991 book, *Self-Made in America*, is still selling. John McCormack is a man alert to possibilities.

The Five Essentials of Life

There are many possibilities in your life. To take advantage of them, you need five things.

1. *Something to do:* a job, a passion, something to study, a cause to work for, a garden to dig in, a marathon to train for.

2. *Someone to love:* your mate, parents, siblings, children, friends, pets.

3. *People to share with:* all of your loved ones, plus business associates, people with whom you have common interests and enthusiasms, and acquaintances in every walk of life.

4. *People to challenge you:* role models, mentors, cronies, students, apprentices, children, and, especially, people who disagree with you and therefore help you grow.

5. *Something to look forward to:* personal growth, positive changes, a seminar, a book, a vacation, a movie, a picnic.

Sleeping in Your Car

How many people do *you* know who would be willing to live in their cars for a year and a half so they could pursue their dream? Would you do it?

Terry Jaymes did. His dream was to work in communications. "I've always known I wanted to be in the entertainment field, either as an actor or a sports announcer, in front of the microphone or behind. A lot of the people I grew up with, friends and family, still don't know what they want to do. When I see them going through that, I realize how lucky I am. Everything in my life seems like a miracle."

After high school, Terry was working late at night at a supermarket, cleaning floors, but he needed some fun and direction in his life. "The local junior college basketball team in my area was the number one team in the nation." The courses were Terry's ticket into the classes taught by the team's coach. What with the academic classes, basketball, and his job, Terry had little time left for traveling from one to the other. "Sometimes, I'd wake up in my car because I'd worked all night, gotten off work at 8:00 a.m., and not bothered to go home because I'd have a class at noon. I always found ways to make it to basketball class.

"One day the coach asked me why I didn't go out for the team. 'Are you kidding?' I said, 'You guys are great.' He says,

'What size shoe do you wear?' I told him and he came back with four pairs. 'You're on the team. Practice is today at 3:30.'"

Everyone on the team got college basketball scholarship offers. Because of this, Terry was able to pursue what he really wanted to do, radio and television. Although he was never a great basketball player, he did get to play in Australia several times.

Consistent and relentless pursuit of your goals requires you to explore all opportunities. Although Terry knew he'd never have a career in basketball, he used it as a way to achieve his ambition. Every opportunity, no matter how unrelated it may seem to your goals, can be a chance to open doors that lead to where you really want to go.

After college, Terry got a job working late at night for a small radio station in San Bernardino, California, that played nothing but Barry Manilow and religious music. Although this was far from his dream job, Terry used it as a springboard to bigger things. While visiting a friend in Santa Barbara, he heard a rock station he liked, so he submitted an audition tape.

Terry was relentless about getting this first big job. He called the program director practically every day. Months later, when the director finally gave Terry a job, she told him that although he was not yet the best, he certainly was the most persistent. To make ends meet, he took a day job at a tennis resort. His total monthly income was about $200. Then the tennis club closed. Rather than give up his radio job, he moved into his car, taking showers at the nearby university locker room. He was constantly promised full-time radio jobs, but none of them worked out.

"I loved radio. I knew I wasn't very good yet, but I also knew I didn't want to leave. I'd take a stack of records into a production room late at night and practice doing a radio show. I'd read the copy and play the commercials over and over. Nobody heard me, but I figured it was the only way I was going to get better. After a year and a half, I finally got a full-time job. That's when everything started to roll. For one thing, I met some comedians and started doing comedy and acting. It snowballed once I got my confidence up."

Terry's ongoing struggle mirrors the seesaw of success and setbacks that all talented performers face. He has appeared in national commercials, had a recurring part on the soap opera "Santa Barbara," and has a spot in a Kris Kristofferson film that may never be released. He hosted a show called "Pure Insanity" for Fox Network, a show that aired only twice. Currently he's syndicated through KTXQ Radio in Dallas to many markets. Like every achiever, Terry makes a few steps forward, one step back.

"But all along, knowing what I wanted was the main thing, just trusting and knowing it would happen. I know exactly where I want to go right now. I know my final goals. There's no doubt in my mind it will happen. There's no fear. I can feel what I'll be wearing, the temperature in the room. I want it so bad I can't wait. But I've learned patience. It will happen when it happens, and in the meantime I'll be doing everything I can to make it happen."

Terry Jaymes may not yet be a national household name, but with that kind of dedication, it's only a matter of time!

Inspiring Others with Your Possibilities

Chances are, you've seen Clare Revelli's TV infomercials or you own or have made a gift of one of her fashion products or hit books, like *Color & You*, *Style & You*, and *Design & You*. But Clare almost lost her big break—until luck and convincing others of her possibilities gave her the boost she needed.

Before Clare started her own business, she worked as director of special events at the Emporium-Capwell department store, where, in 1979, she presented the country's first career program for women. It did very well. Macy's recruited her for a similar position. After a year with them, she decided to start her own business.

Clare took a sabbatical and wrote her first book based on the Seasonal Color Concept, a course she had been teaching at the Fashion Institute of Design and Merchandising and at San Francisco State University. Her first book, *Color & You*, came out in 1982, self-published so she could retain full control over the color reproductions. Clare designed and wrote it as a marketing tool to explain her concept and, eventually, to sell related products. The last page of the book was a mail order form which her firm used to accumulate mailing lists.

Until the early 1980's, Clare had a little office on Union Street and one employee, who was paid when the money came in. Then *Woman's Day*, the second largest women's magazine in the country, asked her to design a color analysis kit for their readers. For $19.95, a woman could fill out the "Revelli Color Analysis Questionnaire" in the magazine, and receive a customized Revelli color kit. Each kit contained a suede wallet, the Revelli Personal Palette, fabric swatches, and a three-page letter of advice about the colors best suited for her wardrobe, accessories and cosmetics. The kit also included a national brands make-up guide and a copy of Clare's book, *Color & You*. Because of their huge readership, *Woman's Day* asked Clare to prepare approximately ten thousand kits in advance. That involved an enormous amount of money up front. Clare describes the obstacles she faced.

"I was a single woman renting a small apartment here in San Francisco and had only a fifteen-year-old car for collateral on a bank loan. Not much, right? I needed $25,000 start-up money, but every bank I approached turned me down.

"Then, as fashion editor for the *Nob Hill Gazette*—I always had freelance jobs on the side—I was covering the opening of the new Louis Vuitton store in San Francisco when I struck up a conversation with a nice woman. She turned out to be a loan officer at a local bank! We found we had a lot in common. She also was a native San Franciscan of Italian origin—and we decided to have lunch together the following week.

"On Monday I called her at the bank to arrange lunch. At first she couldn't place me, then suddenly she said, 'Oh, yes, you're the fashion editor who needs a bank loan.' By the time I took her to lunch, she had looked over my financial records and noticed I had no collateral. She said, 'There's only one way you're going to get a loan. Do exactly what I tell you. I'll wait to inform my bosses upstairs that I'm putting your loan through until I've already given you the money. Now, fill out these forms. Your loan will be rejected, but it will be too late. I really believe in you and your program, so I'm willing to take this chance.'

"The next morning, on her instructions, I went to her bank and withdrew the $25,000 I needed to set up the Woman's Day kits. The day after that, her bosses did in fact stamp 'rejected' on my loan application, telling her it was 'fraught with peril'!

"The *Woman's Day* promotion was successful beyond my wildest dreams. When it broke on the newsstands, we got approximately 8,000 orders in the first ten days. By the time the program finished a year and a half later—and mind you this was a one-time February issue—they had received over 30,000 orders at $20 per order. Everyone involved made a great deal of money."

Clare could still be organizing department store fashion shows and Easter egg hunts (and that's not a bad thing to be doing), but because she believed in her own possibilities and got others to believe in them, she achieved much, much more. Clare's *Color & You* (Simon & Schuster) has sold 3 million copies to date. In addition, she has written promotional books on hair coloring: *Colors of Your Life* for Clairol, which has sold 50,000 copies; *Color Sense for No Nonsense* with 4 million copies; and more recently *Focus on Color* for Ralston Purina, 2 million copies so far.

Clare also has an assortment of licensees for scarves, eyeglasses, belts, jewelry, and even a software computer program. All products are nationally distributed and labeled with the Revelli name.

And if all this were not enough, she has licensed her name to a video based on her book, *Color & You*. The video is marketed by Simon & Schuster and distributed by Paramount. Clare's latest venture is a television pilot, *Design & You*.

Some people would call Clare lucky, but it's the kind of luck we've been talking about—the luck that doesn't happen unless you are out there plugging away, exploring your possibilities. "I've been through ups and downs as most people have," says Clare, "but I always listen to my inner voice. I have great faith things will always work out." Clare recognized her possibilities and convinced others to back her. Her contract with *Woman's Day* magazine and her chance meeting with the bank loan officer were opportunities for her to succeed, opportunities to which she said "yes."

Possibilities in a New Land

Nicole Schapiro was just a baby when her parents were imprisoned in a concentration camp during World War II. Friends hid the child throughout the war. Miraculously, both her parents survived, and they went in search of Nicole. When they found her, the beautiful, bouncy baby girl they had left eight years before had become a mute, withdrawn nine-year-old.

Desperate for anything that would help restore the bright, energetic child she remembered, Nicole's mother sent her to mime school. About the same time, Nicole found an old book about America in the basement of her home in Hungary, a book full of marvelous stories about this distant country. The Communist regime had made it illegal to possess anything printed by American publishers, but Nicole treasured this book and read the stories over and over. She decided she was going to be an American.

In 1957, the Hungarian Revolution broke out, and Nicole learned how to make Molotov cocktails. She was caught along with twenty-one other young people and lined up with them to be shot. Nicole was fifteen, and the executioners were no older. Of the group, only Nicole survived. When she looks back she asks herself, "How come?" She remembers that, for a single instant, she and the Russian soldier looked at each other as he raised his rifle to kill her. They seemed to think together that "This is crazy, why are we doing this?"

He didn't kill her, and she escaped, more determined than ever to leave for America. But the American consulate said the quota was frozen. America didn't want any more Hungarians. So she spent one month standing in front of the consulate until she became an eyesore. Finally, they decided, "She really wants to go."

Eventually she appealed to President Eisenhower. She wrote, "We both have the same vision. We both love America and want it to be a free and equal country. Freedom is not that we are able to get everything we want. Freedom is that you can become whatever you want to become. What I can do, if you let me in, is I will be able to influence people. I want to influence people all over the world to feel like you do."

Life in the land of opportunity has had both boosts and bumps for Nicole. She sought the chance to do the best she could do, to make a difference for herself and others. She has been a vice president of sales and marketing for Citibank in New York. She has also survived cancer and rebuilt her life after the devastating 1991 Oakland Hills fire destroyed her home, her business records, and the manuscript of a book she was writing. Today she is healthy, the author of *Negotiating for Your Life*, a fund-raiser for cancer research, and a top speaker and seminar leader influencing people around the country—just as she promised Eisenhower she would.

In her handsome renovated house across the bay in Sausalito, Nicole keeps an onion on her desk. Once when she was a little girl, her mother had been too poor to make her a birthday cake. Instead they took an onion and pretended it was a cake. Now the onion reminds her of where she's been and of the opportunities that open up when you are alert to the possibilities.

YOUR ASSIGNMENT:
What Are My Possibilities?

FRIPPICISM

Keep yourself constantly open to possibilities.

Three things I'd really like to do, but which are absolutely, utterly impossible are:

1._____

2._____

3._____

Three things I'd really like to do that would be easy if I just tried are:

1._____

2._____

3._____

What items from the impossible list do I want to reconsider?

What items from the easy list do I want to go for?

CHAPTER 15

Making Things Happen

> **FRIPPICISM**
>
> *"Ordinary" people can make extraordinary things happen.*

When you go to work each day, how do you think about what's ahead? Do you think, "I've got sixteen customers to deal with"? Or do you think, "I've got sixteen opportunities to transform people's lives"? Do you say, "I'll be spending eight hours shuffling papers" (or flipping hamburgers, bagging groceries, answering phones, or greeting patients)? Or do you think, "I'll be spending eight hours as an indispensable part of a terrific team that makes people happier, healthier, or more prosperous and the world a better place"?

What are the chances that people who choose the former responses will make a powerful difference in other people's lives? And what are the chances that people with a passionate, positive vision of what they do will *fail* to make such a difference?

Make Your Own Breaks

When you're starting out—and this goes whether you're starting out at twenty or starting over at sixty—take on *anything*. Once I was on a program with Joan Lunden, then with "Good

Morning, America," who told me her classic "only in America" story. She'd been a meteorologist at local stations in New York and California when she got her big break because her boss was sick. She filled in as a newscaster, was noticed, and accepted a job with the network. At first, she was given a lot of small assignments, hardly the prestigious broadcasting career she had dreamed about. Many people would have gotten discouraged, but Barbara Walters offered her some great advice: "Take every crumb they throw at you, and handle each magnificently." Lunden knew precisely what she wanted to become. She saw these petty jobs as paying her dues and learning her craft so she'd be ready for the really big time. She made her own breaks, using her clear vision.

Market Yourself Shamelessly

Merv Adelson, who, coincidentally, was married to Barbara Walters at the time, was in the audience when I spoke at a teleconferencing event he co-produced. Afterwards, this very busy, important Hollywood executive personally picked up the phone and called to compliment me. Sometime later, when I was in Southern California on business, I called his secretary back and said, "Mr. Adelson was so nice to me. Is there any chance I could come by and just meet him for a few minutes?" I ended up having a twenty-five minute meeting with him. He was very gracious. At one point, he commented, "My wife gives talks too."

"Yes," I said. "I just quoted her in one I gave." Adelson laughed. "Every time Barbara wants something special, like a coat or a piece of furniture, she gives a speech to get the money." What stands out in my mind from my conversation with Mr. Adelson is that, even though Barbara Walters makes millions a year, if something seems extravagant, she justifies it by doing something extra to get the money. I hope I stand out in Adelson's mind as someone who really appreciated his giving me some of his time.

Forging Steel Magnolias

Jeanne Robertson is the kind of person who really gets going when she's told, "it can't be done." Jeanne (pronounced Jee-nee) is an old hand at making things happen, both for herself and for others. She's been a speaker for thirty-five years and is past president of the National Speakers Association. Without a doubt, she's the best humorist on the speaking circuit, working harder than anyone I know to stay fresh at her craft. Here's how she simultaneously fulfilled a secret desire and benefited her North Carolina community.

"In 1989," says Jeanne, "the movie version of *Steel Magnolias* came out, and it was hot! It's about southern women, and everyone was seeing it and talking about it. I decided I'd really love to be in a stage production of the play. A friend, Linda Pulliam, commented she would too. We could just see ourselves. We weren't really actresses, but I'd been in a high school play, and Linda had acted in some things years ago.

"However, we assumed our chances of working with a little theater group were near zero because we thought you had to hammer nails and change scenery before they'd let you act. Still, I checked out some local theaters to see if they were eager for fledgling actresses. Well, you'd be amazed how many talented, experienced actresses there are in North Carolina, fighting for roles! No one walks up to you at a party and shouts, 'Stop everything, we're going to put you in a play!' It doesn't work that way." The matter seemed settled, for the time being.

Soon afterwards, Jeanne and her buddy Linda learned that while they had been preoccupied with their speaking careers, *Steel Magnolias* had been performed at a nearby theater. They were disappointed to have missed the show and reminded again of their dream to appear on stage...some day.

Years went by, filled with packed schedules that kept the theater dream on the back burner. Then, in the fall of 1995, Jeanne was in New York and went to see Edward Albee's play *Three Tall Women* with two friends. Jeanne recalls her reaction. "That was it. A woman who makes her living on the stage giving speeches was bitten by the play bug." The height of the women appealed to Jeanne, who stands six foot two, but even more, she was gripped by the dynamism of the actresses and their ability to bring such enjoyment to their audience. At intermission, she turned to her friends and said, "I want to do this!" Both were astonished.

"Why would you want to?"

"I don't know, but I'm going to find a way." Jeanne's friends, like any good cronies, supported her in her enthusiasm. The next week, one of them sent her the script as a gift, with a note, "See if you can do it." Jeanne saw another production of *Three Tall Women* a few months later while in Los Angeles, and this time she could no longer resist the call. Back in North Carolina, she telephoned local theater groups to learn how she might fit stage acting into her speaking career. She asked each group the same three questions and got the same answers.

Q: Do you ever cast a play eight or ten months in advance so I could try out and, if cast, not book speaking engagements for the show dates?
A: No, we cast four to six weeks before performance and immediately go into rehearsal.

Q: Do you ever perform a play over Christmas, which is a slow time for me?
A: No.

Q: Would you consider it?
A: Why? No one does plays then. People are too busy to come.

Jeanne hung up and called Holt Skinner, a young man active in community theater who had gone to school with her son. "What does it cost to produce a play, and how do you go about it?" she asked. "Tell me all." Holt and Jeanne began meeting to explore producing a play the following year, a fund-raiser with proceeds going to benefit the major local theater group. They decided that *Three Tall Women*, although a terrific play, wouldn't work in their area even if they could obtain the performance rights. "People think of me as a funny person," says Jeanne, "someone they can bring their children to hear speak, and you really couldn't take children to such a serious work."

That's when Jeanne's attention turned back to the play that had ignited her interest, *Steel Magnolias*. Audiences had loved it, and it was now almost seven years since it had been performed in the area. "I certainly had the Southern accent down pat," says Jeanne, "and we agreed it would be the perfect vehicle."

In the meantime, without knowing of a possible play in the works, the Alamance County Arts Council approached Jeanne about becoming the honorary chairman for its upcoming campaign to raise $1.5 million. The money would go toward renovating two historic structures. One was a former private home, which would become the headquarters for the arts in the area. The other happened to be the old downtown theater used by the group Holt and Jeanne were considering as recipient of their fund-raiser. "I'll do it if I can really be involved," said Jeanne.

Suddenly Jeanne saw the perfect match. She could fulfill her secret dream while helping her community. The Arts Council agreed. The campaign kicked off in September, with the play scheduled for the two weeks after Christmas—the time when nay-sayers had predicted no one would have time to come. Big contributors were invited to a special preview night with a gala after the play. A local benefactor underwrote production costs, so every penny from ticket sales could go to the Arts Campaign.

Because the play was being billed around Jeanne's local celebrity, she was cast first. Although a tragedy in her own family made the character of M'Lynn (played by Sally Field in the movie) especially moving for her, Jeanne was persuaded that the humorous and shorter part of Ouiser (Shirley MacLaine in the movie) was best suited to her talents and available time.

Auditions were held in August, again a time that nay-sayers had said was too early to cast a local production. Jeanne called Linda, who was out of state on vacation, and urged her to come back and try out. "We've been talking about this for years. You at least have to give it a shot!" Linda returned and auditioned without telling the producer and director she and Jeanne were friends. She was cast as Clairee (Olympia Dukakis in the film). Jeanne and Linda not only were going to realize their dream, but they would realize it together! Four strong actresses from the area were cast in the other roles.

The group rehearsed all autumn, working around each other's schedules. The local college theater wasn't available until December, so the newly formed troupe cleared the game room in Jeanne's home and constructed a makeshift set for rehearsals. Jeanne and Linda continued giving speeches until the week before Thanksgiving, then stopped to devote full time to the production.

Using marketing expertise developed through her speaking career and her experiences with the National Speakers Association, Jeanne drew up three pages of promotion ideas, designed to fill the theater every night. These included giving free speeches at senior citizens' events and local clubs to promote the campaign and play, as well as doing TV, radio, and cable appearances. The six cast members did a one-hour radio talk show, discussing how their individual characters grew as women during the play.

"We tried to come up with every possible promotional angle. For example, in the play, one character has a diabetic attack. People from the American Diabetes Society advised us on how to handle that scene. Then we got a feature story in the health section of the local paper about diabetes, and under it a smaller story about the play. At the theater each night, we handed out material from the Society."

In the movie, there was an armadillo cake, so they got one donated and used that publicity. The character who dies is a member of the Phi Mu sorority, so members of the local chapter were invited to come as a group. The fund raisers also approached companies about having Christmas or New Year's Eve parties at the play combined with dinner at a nearby restaurant. "We had more ideas than we had time to use," says Jeanne. Working with a local public relations firm, Jeanne generated publicity for the other cast members. The campaign contacted every newspaper and magazine in the area, giving each an exclusive story. Through a friend, they invited Margaret Harling, the real-life woman on whom the M'Lynn character is based and the mother of the playwright, Robert Harling. She and a friend flew to North Carolina to attend the play and a reception. She graciously gave interviews and appeared on local radio while she was there. "This was exciting for us beyond words, and excellent publicity."

Steel Magnolias sold out every night but New Year's day, when there were scattered empty seats. It cleared $31,000, not counting opening night revenues where each seat went for a $5,000 donation to the Arts Council. In addition to helping raise $1.3 million, the production provided an exciting vehicle for keeping the campaign in the news for many months.

Jeanne's goal seemed nearly impossible at first, but she took charge and went ahead. "When we started, I didn't know how to do everything," says Jeanne, "but I was determined, and so I learned. You have to ignore the nay-sayers, take a deep breath, and decide *you* can make things happen."

Don't Be Normal

Tony Jones went to work for my father when he was sixteen, became his partner, and took over the business when my father retired. Recently, I had lunch with Tony who razzed me, "What is it about all you Fripps? None of you are normal!"

I'm not sure what I will do with the next fifty years of my life, but I do know I don't want to be "normal." Normal people don't celebrate their birthdays all year round. Normal people don't want to be on billboards or live the lifestyle of the rich and famous or get inspired by John Travolta movies. I do get inspiration from movies. Frank Sinatra once told Shirley MacLaine, "When you walk in a room, make a difference." Most people don't think they do. But each of us is capable of weaving our own special magic. To make things happen, decide you don't want to be normal!

Getting Others Started

There are two kinds of people who make things happen: those who think up great ideas and those who are inspired to carry them out.

Some people come up with a big idea and set it up so well that others can take the concept and run with it. Dan Maddux is one of them. He's the long-time executive director of the dynamic American Payroll Association (APA), one of the thousands of trade and professional organizations designed to inform and promote their members.

Maddux wanted citizens to be more aware of the behind-the-scenes contributions of payroll workers. His most recent Big Idea was National Payroll Week. How many of us spend more than a few seconds a week (if that) thinking about payrolls? Yet the economy of the entire civilized world would grind to a halt without the talented, efficient people who process them.

Once Maddux had the idea for National Payroll Week, one of his first steps was to approach the White House for support. He got it. White House staff worked closely with Maddux and APA's Government Affairs Director Carolyn Kelley during the months before September 16-20, 1996, coordinating support from government agencies such as the IRS, Social Security Administration, and the Department of Labor. National Payroll Week was quickly picked up by the media, and local chapters worked hard to make it a success at every level. Many prominent corporations and associations came forward as sponsors, and President Bill Clinton sent a letter of commendation and support. As a result, millions of people today are much more conscious of the critical contribution of America's payroll workers.

Maddux knows not everyone has the time, talent, contacts, drive, and wherewithal to start a big project, but many people are eager to make their own contribution once they're inspired and shown how. The project's catalyst person and those who keep it going are responsible for making it happen.

Donors and Doers

Whenever there's a worthwhile idea, some people can write a check for $10,000 without blinking, while others say, "I'll give you $10,000 worth of time and energy." What makes an idea come alive is that real people, people who don't fly in corporate jets, take it up and run with it, sometimes in ways the originator didn't envision.

You don't have to be the one who starts something in order to make a difference. Often it's more efficient to let someone else figure everything out and then pass it off to you. My former assistant Becky Gordon read about a grassroots all-volunteer project to make sleeping bags for the homeless out of recycled materials that otherwise would become landfill.

In 1985, a nurse named Flo Wheatley from Hop Bottom, Pennsylvania visited Manhattan and was horrified to see people living on the streets and suffering from potentially fatal hypothermia. Most of us have seen such tragic incidents of local and global suffering, and felt helpless. What can one person do to solve such overwhelming and complex problems? It's easier to turn away and think of something pleasant. However, Flo Wheatley decided someone had to start somewhere. She went home and sewed old blankets and leftovers from the church rummage sale into a simple sleeping bag. The first year, she made and distributed eight bags. Her neighbors asked what she was doing, and they began to help too. Slowly the project grew and spread until, in 1997, more than 100,000 free sleeping bags had been handed out all across the U.S., and the project had sprung up in a dozen other countries.

This is where Becky joins the story. In 1995 she heard about the project. Even though San Francisco never has snow, it does have cold nights, and an estimated 8,000 to 20,000 homeless people, more than a hundred of whom die each year on the streets. Becky recognized that "My Brother's Keeper," as the project is called, would be a great use of her sewing and organizing skills. She formed a San Francisco core group that has turned out nearly 300 sleeping bags. In addition, the group does demonstrations showing church, senior, and youth groups how to make the simple bags. The San Francisco volunteers have produced an all-volunteer, five-minute instructional video that proved so popular and useful that more than 10,000 have been distributed nationwide.

Becky is a busy businesswoman who would never have had the time to conceive of and start such an innovative project. But, joining a project initiated by someone else, she and her fellow volunteers can donate their time and energy whenever possible, keenly aware their efforts may literally save a life.

You Have to Ask

One of my own claims to fame is that I raised $30,000 for the Leukemia Society of America in one month. People who've been involved in fund-raising often ask me, "How'd you do that?" My answer is: "I asked."

One of the best salespeople I ever met phoned me at 5:30 one afternoon. Her name is Liz Hills, and she said, "I hear you're a mover, a shaker, a wheeler, and a dealer."

"You heard right," I said.

"How would you like to raise money for the Leukemia Society in a contest?"

"I have absolutely no interest whatsoever," I said.

Being a good salesperson, Liz kept talking. "Let me tell you what you get if you win this contest," she said. "Your picture will be featured on ten billboards in San Francisco." Now doesn't that sound like something an unashamed, relentless self-promoter might be interested in? I'd always had a hankering to promote my hairstyling business with some nice billboards, but could never afford them. Still, I continued to imagine myself up there, smiling down on the city.

I knew she had me. Still, I played hard to get. I said, "Look, I'm tired, crabby, and bad-tempered." (Even motivational speakers get tired, crabby and bad-tempered.) I said, "I'm not saying yes, but if you send me the information, I promise to read it when I'm not tired." When it came, I discovered that during the six weeks until the contest deadline, I would be out of town traveling all but five days.

Other people were putting on big fundraising events like parties and golf tournaments. I realized I didn't have the time to do that, so instead I wrote letters to all my friends:

Have I ever done you a favor, given you advice, or recommended you for a speaking engagement, knitted you a sweater, invited you to a fun party, sent money to your favorite charity, or come to your wedding with a gift but stayed single myself? Do you like me? Do you support the work of the Leukemia Society of America? ....I've always wanted to be on billboards and this is such a good cause.

P.S. I hope you don't think I did nice things for you because I planned to ask you for money. But please send it anyway.

Never in my life have I felt so loved as when I saw all those envelopes coming back with checks and notes saying things like, "Patricia, my business really isn't doing very well right now, but you've always supported me, so I want to support you."

As I have mentioned, I believe life is a series of sales situations. Whatever you're promoting—yourself, your business, your philosophy, or a good cause—the answer is "no" if you don't ask. Sometimes you ask and the answer is still "no," but I guarantee it's *always* "no" if you don't ask.

I'm the first to admit I went into that contest because I wanted to be on billboards. I was prepared to do the work and not win, but I did win, and I'm happy to tell you I have milked the fact to death. I've had the photo of me on that billboard printed on tee-shirts, postcards, and stationery. I confess my involvement with the Leukemia Society has been a useful credential to get speaking engagements with nonprofit associations. But I also confess I got emotionally involved and still work with them, though in a less flashy role. I now co-chair the same campaign each year, and help other chapters in their fund-raising and recruiting for the Woman and Man of the Year contests in other cities.

We held a big party next to one of my billboards. A local clothing store was a corporate sponsor, so I had asked them, "Will you send some people to blow up the balloons? Will you donate champagne and pour it?" It was a wonderful party, and the charity, the corporate sponsor, and I all got great publicity. All my friends from the National Speakers Association turned up in tee-shirts with a picture of the billboard, and they sang "There's no billboard like Fripp's billboard." A friend, Paula Statman, came up with "The Fripp Rap" or "Give Me Your Money."

I received an official proclamation presented by a politician! I had asked the charity, "Will you ask the mayor to proclaim it Patricia Fripp Day in San Francisco?" (People will do almost anything if you just ask!) So I got a proclamation. Then I said, "I'd like a city official to come by and give it to me so we can have a photo opportunity to put on video." President of the Board of Supervisors, Angela Alioto, dropped by the party and presented it to me. Any politician running for office will go anywhere for seven minutes, make a speech, and give you a proclamation if you have a crowd. Everybody wins.

Moral: *Anytime you can promote yourself and do something good at the same time, do it.*

YOUR ASSIGNMENT:
What Will I Make Happen?

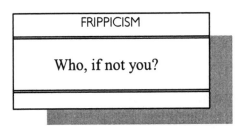

FRIPPICISM

Who, if not you?

Three (or more) things I'd like to make happen are:

_____

_____

_____

Which of these will I choose to work on first?

What will I do to make a difference?

Homework Assignment

Decide on a special reward you'll give yourself as soon as you've accomplished one of the things on your list above.

CHAPTER 16

Speak Out

> ### FRIPPICISM
>
> *It doesn't matter how good you are. The world has to know it.*

Outside the privacy of your own home, all speaking is public speaking. There is no such thing as "private speaking." If you can stand up and speak eloquently and with confidence, or if you can stagger to your feet and say anything at all, you will be head and shoulders above your competition.

Visibility is necessary to succeed in almost any business, and people who can speak clearly and eloquently impress others as superior. If you can address a group, that is a big plus. But just having the confidence to discuss your views with others gives you an edge over your competition.

Chances are, you haven't had sufficient preparation for convincing and tactful self-expression. In the old days, debating was part of every school's curriculum. Students learned how to discuss all sides of an issue without losing their tempers or respect for their opponents. If you were born too late for these valuable lessons, consider enrolling in a public speaking class or joining Toastmasters.

Your personal life can benefit too. If you sometimes come down with foot-in-mouth disease when you try to discuss sensitive issues with family members, you can improve personal communications by learning how to "do a presentation"—to persuade, offer a plan, or express your point of view. If you routinely get flustered, angry, or even tearful during intimate discussions, or if you avoid them entirely because of the discomfort, consider developing your speaking skills.

Everyone has knowledge and experience to share. If you clam up with nerves in a PTA meeting, a church group, or a staff meeting, you are not sharing your knowledge with other people or contributing to the group decision process. Even though you may not wish to become a professional speaker, there is no greater confidence booster in the world than being able to speak comfortably in front of others.

I recommend public speaking for everyone. What I want to help you with in the rest of this chapter is serious, organized, planned public speaking, the kind that brings you or your organization prestige, publicity, money and other good things. First, I'll tell you how to put together speeches you can use to increase the visibility of your business. If you're not in business for yourself, you may still find this section useful for presentations of any kind.

Promote Yourself

One of the best ways to promote your product or service and expand your customer base is also one of the cheapest. Interested? It's public speaking. I know this from first-hand experience. I started talking about my hairstyling business at local service organizations, such as the Rotary, Kiwanis, and Optimists clubs. My first speech was called "Miracles and Men's Hair." Often, after I spoke at a client's 8:00 a.m. sales meeting, three members of the audience would book haircutting appointments for lunchtime.

What I've compiled for you is a one-chapter version of some of the most important things I've learned in the last twenty years that might be useful for any shaking-in-their-boots but eager-to-enhance-their-business non-speakers.

What to Talk About

Start by asking yourself three questions:

1. Who is my audience? (What do I know about the corporate culture or collective personality of the group?)

2. What do they want or need to know?

3. How long can or should I talk?

How to Outline Your Talk

There are two basic outlines that work well for beginning speakers.

The AA Way: Alcoholics Anonymous has an effective outline for its members to stand up and "qualify" their experiences:

- This is where I was.
- This is where I am.
- This is how I got here.

It's a simple format that helps you tell the audience who you are and why you are qualified to speak on the topic you've chosen.

Here's an example of how effective the AA outline can be. A successful Realtor was asked to do a 25-minute presentation for the local Board of Realtors. I suggested she open like this: "Twelve years ago, before I went into the real estate business, I had never sold anything but Girl Scout cookies, and I hadn't done that well. Last year, I sold $13 million in a slow market, selling homes that averaged $100,000 each. Today, I'll tell you how I built my business." Right away, the audience knew exactly what she was going to talk about, and they were all ears to hear her story!

The Q&A format: The members of your audience probably want to know the answers to the same kinds of business questions you're asked at cocktail parties or professional functions. You can start with, "The five questions I'm most frequently asked about investments (or engineering or whatever your product or service is) are..."

Pose the first question to the audience and answer it for them in a conversational manner, just as you would a potential customer or someone you meet at a party. Even though you've never made a speech before, you've certainly had a lot of experience answering questions in your field.

How to Write Your Speech

That's easy. To begin with, don't. Gather and organize your material, plan and polish, but don't write it down word for word. You'll do that later. For now, just jot an outline with key lines and ideas on a note pad.

As you brainstorm for effective material, don't worry at first about where it will go. This process benefits from some downtime. Start in plenty of time if you can, and keep your notepad handy. With time, you'll find your ideas fitting into a natural sequence. Juggle them around until you are satisfied. Now you can begin to write.

FRIPPICISM

Your first thirty seconds and your last thirty seconds have the most impact. Come out punching, and leave them on a high.

The Start of Your Speech

Start strong. Psychologists have proven that if you don't grab attention in the first thirty seconds, you probably won't.

You don't have the luxury of four minutes as you do in a one-on-one encounter. If you haven't hooked your audience's interest within half a minute, their minds are going to wander off to shopping lists, uncomfortable shoes, or what they should have said at the meeting that afternoon.

Never start by saying, "Ladies and gentlemen, it's a pleasure to be here." It's a weak, rather meaningless thought, and it wastes too much of your precious thirty seconds.

The conventional wisdom is to start with a joke. Do so *only* if it reflects your personality and is the natural launching pad for your subject. Test each of your possibilities by asking:

- Is it appropriate for the occasion and the audience?
- Is it in good taste?
- Does it relate to me (my product or service)?
- Does it support my topic or its key points?

It's usually easier and safer to start by giving the audience the information they most want to hear. For example, I helped a neighbor, Mike Powell, with a speech he was putting together for the Continental Breakfast Club in San Francisco. At the time, Mike was a senior scientist with Genentech. I said, "Mike, most people don't hang around with scientists, and even if they do, they don't understand what they are talking about. Tell them what it is like so they understand." So Mike told them:

Being a scientist is like doing a jigsaw puzzle—in a snowstorm—at night—when you don't have all the pieces—and you don't have a picture of what you are trying to create.

Mike immediately captured everyone's attention. Keep your opening compact. You can say more with less.

The Middle of Your Speech

Here's where you expand on your key points. In the AA outline format, you develop personal stories that support where you were and are. For the Q&A format, develop one or two stories to support the answers for each of your questions. If your audience is here to learn about your business, you'll probably be able to predict what information they want most. If you're not sure, talk to the program chair.

The End of Your Speech

End strong. The close should be the highlight of your speech. The last thirty seconds of your speech has to send people off energized and fulfilled. Summarize the key points you've made. If you're going to take questions, try saying, "Before my closing remarks, are there any questions?" You want to leave your audience with something more memorable than a Q&A session. Then finish your talk with something inspirational that supports your theme.

Remember, it's no sin to finish early but definitely bad form to run late. It shows you have little consideration for the organization, the program chair, and the audience. If, after you finish, they ask you to continue beyond your scheduled time, that's a different story.

After my scientist friend told our group of the frustrations of being a scientist, he closed by saying, "People often ask, 'why would anyone want to be a scientist?'" To answer this question, he told of a particularly information-intensive medical conference he had attended. The last speaker of the day stepped up to the lectern and said, "I am a 32-year-old wife and mother of two. I have AIDS. Please work fast."

Emotional or dramatic material works well for a closing. It is good to leave your audience with something to think about.

Add the I-You Factor

Be sure you've connected yourself with your audience by putting them into your speech. For instance, suppose you're talking about financial planning and you say:

> *I always pay myself first. Not the recommended 10 percent. I save 20 percent of my gross income.*

Your audience will probably be rolling their eyes and thinking, "Yeah, *right*..." But if, instead, you say:

> *The American Dream is fast becoming a nightmare. Now, more than ever before, we need to save 10 percent of our income. You may be thinking, "Oh, yeah, you don't know my paycheck!" No, I don't, but I promise you, the secret to sleeping well at night is to save something...anything...on a regular basis. Even 1 percent compounded may be the difference between winning and losing. Here are my three recommendations for a good night's sleep and growing old with a solid, secure future.*

Some other phrases that help to add the I-You factor are:

- Have you ever thought...
- You remember when...
- Come with me...
- Imagine...
- Have you ever read...
- Did you see...
- You know how, when you...

This puts the audience in your speech. Instead of scoffing, they are more likely to identify with what you're saying.

Edit, Edit, Edit

Practice with a tape recorder to get some idea of timing and emphasis. You think that's too much trouble for a free speech? Maybe, but you'll be glad you did. Then have your words transcribed. When you read your transcript, look for:

Who-cares material—Did you go off on a tangent that doesn't relate to your theme? Did you offer an example that fell short?

Redundancies—Are you saying the same thing three different ways? Eliminate phrases like "new beginnings," "free gifts," and "true facts."

Non-words—"er," "ah."

Repetitive phrases—"Now...," "You know..."

Clichés—"Without further ado," "the rubber chicken circuit," "that's a tough act to follow." There are countless clichés in every industry. Get rid of them.

Cross out nonessential words and phrases. Your talk will be tighter and more effective. Since your own extra verbiage can be hard to spot, it can be helpful to ask a friend to listen to your tape or read your transcript and help with the weeding.

Practice, Practice, Practice

You've edited and fine-tuned a written version of your talk. Now practice it, first alone and then in front of an audience of one or two people for their feedback. Make it clear you want sincere feedback, not just praise. Did they understand the points you were making? Was there a lack of logic or continuity? Did they think you spoke too quickly or slowly?

Prepare Your Notes

Even though you've just gone to a great deal of trouble to prepare a written speech, you're not going to use it! Instead, you're going to write your key points on a pad you'll keep on the lectern or table. Use a bold felt-tip pen or a large typeface on your printer.

You'll follow your road map with quick glances, making sure you haven't skipped anything, while maintaining good eye contact with your audience. Remember, the audience has no idea what you intended saying.

Check In Early

Arrive early at the place you'll be speaking so you can check out the logistics.

Microphone—Learn how to turn it on and off and how to remove it from the stand. Practice talking into it. If it's not a cordless mike, practice walking up and down without tangling the cord around your feet.

Audio/Video Equipment—Check any equipment you plan to use—overhead projectors, slide projectors, and VCRs—to be sure it works and you know how to use it. Inspect your slides, transparencies, or videotapes. Are they in the right sequence and in good shape?

Charts—Are chalkboards and flip charts in place and secure? (Toppling easels are a distraction!) Do you have enough blank pages on your flip chart? Plenty of markers? Can you write some of your information ahead of time?

Room Set-up—Where is the platform? Where will you be when you are introduced? What will you have to step over on your way to the mike? Will you need more or less light in the room? Who controls the light switches? (Arrange this ahead of time!) Are seats in the best arrangement for your presentation? A close semicircle works best for an intimate talk with flip charts or chalkboard. Traditional theater-row seating is better if you have slides or videos, but angle the side-most seats forward to increase audience comfort and focus.

Your Introduction—Don't leave anything to chance. Even if you're speaking for free, you want the emcee to pronounce your name right and mention your company's name.

Write your own introduction and give an easy-to-read copy to the emcee. Use your resume as a guide, but customize it to fit the topic. If you've earned or been honored with impressive designations or awards, it's best if the introducer mentions them. Don't list your job as a lifeguard unless it relates to your subject.

Remember those important first thirty seconds. You don't need an introducer who rambles or tells tired jokes. Ideally, you'll be able to arrange with the introducer to remain at the microphone until the audience's attention is fully on you, then get off discretely. Don't be modest about your entrance. No one appreciates a sheepish speaker.

Timing—Keep yourself on schedule, using a travel-style clock on the lectern, or a clearly visible wall clock in the room instead of your watch. (The audience should never be aware you're doing this.)

Don't be surprised if the meeting is running late. Ask the program chair if he or she would like you to cut a few minutes out of your talk to get the event back on schedule. It's not as difficult as you think. Don't sacrifice your strong opening or dramatic closing. Instead, hit the highlights of your talk, dropping some of the supporting stories or anecdotes.

If, on the other hand, the program chair asks you to stretch out your talk, here are some techniques that have worked well for me.

• Always have an extra chunk of material prepared. Perhaps a slightly longer version of a key story or extra supportive stories for each point.

• If you have round-table seating or another suitable format, invite groups discussions on one of your major points.

• If you're teaching a skill, invite someone in the audience to role-play it with you.

• Ask audience members to share their personal experiences relating to your topic (customer service, sales technique, buying real estate, etc.) Then ask, "What did you learn from this experience that you can use in your business?" I offer small prizes to those who speak up—for example, a cassette tape of one of my speeches. This guarantees others in the audience will participate more freely.

Just Before Your Speech

It's time to look your audience in the eye and tell them all the exciting things you know they are eager to hear. If you find a stomach full of butterflies taking some of the joy out of the occasion, here is what the professionals do.

Physical preparation—Find a private place to warm up by relaxing your body and face.

Stand on one leg and shake the other. When you put your foot back on the ground, it's going to feel lighter. Now, switch legs and shake again. It's a technique actors use.

Shake your hands...fast. Hold them above your head, bending at the wrist and elbow, and lower them. This will make your hand movements more natural.

Relax your face muscles by chewing in a highly exaggerated way. Do shoulder and neck rolls.

You are almost ready for the stage.

Deliver Your Speech

I urge you not to stand behind the lectern throughout your entire talk. It puts a barrier between you and the audience, and they feel it. However, if you feel more secure, stand behind it but don't lean on it. Here are a few other pointers on coming across during your moment in the spotlight.

Look the part—Your appearance is the first impression the audience has of you. It can add to your credibility and that of your business.

Act naturally—"What an actor has to do is be personal in public." That's what the famous acting coach Lee Strasberg said. Though being on stage makes you feel larger than life, you also need to be personal in public. That's what all those warm-up exercises are about, helping you to feel and act natural.

Add drama—You're new to speaking and you're not an actor, but you can add excitement to your talk just the same. Once I saw a video of myself at an effective-communications seminar. I thought they were running the video at double speed. The teacher said kindly, "Your strength is your energy, but think of a great symphony. It starts quickly and brightly; then it has a soft, emotional section; and finally it builds to a mighty crescendo. The variety makes each element more effective."

While you're on stage, you want to stand, move, be serious, be funny, talk loudly, talk softly. As my friend Bob Murphey says, "Don't speak in black and white. Speak in Technicolor."

Deal with distractions—During a speech I gave in Australia, one man in the front row took three mobile-phone calls! You can do two things with such distractions: ignore them or use them. My talk in Australia was before 2,000 people, and I chose to ignore the man talking on the phone. I walked purposefully to the side of the stage away from him, bringing the audience's attention with me because eyes follow movement. I worked the crowd there until he was off the phone.

Incorporating the distraction into your talk can be tricky, and it will be different every time. A woman asked my advice about a weekly licensing class she taught at a Holiday Inn. On one occasion, an important football game had been in progress, and members of her audience kept leaving the room for a peek at the giant TV screen in the nearby lobby bar. The comings and goings had been quite disruptive. I suggested that if something like this happened again, she could acknowledge the distraction by saying, "If I didn't have to work here tonight, I probably would be next door watching the football game too. If you don't need the information I'm offering so you can pass the exam, then you can leave with my blessing. But for the benefit of those who want to learn without distractions, please don't disrupt the class by coming back." By acknowledging the situation and graciously allowing the football fanatics to leave, she could get the rest of the audience on her side.

Promote Your Business

When the entire point of your public speaking is to increase awareness of your business and expand your client base, make the most of opportunities to market yourself. Here are my most successful ploys.

Handouts—Develop an informational page or tip sheet. If you've had an article published, make copies for audience members. Make sure the handout includes your name, address, and telephone number. You might also include an order blank for your product or service printed on the back of one of your handouts.

Business cards—If your goal is to develop business contacts, always collect business cards from the audience members. You can offer to send additional information, articles, or tip sheets to them. One good way to get everyone's card is to collect them, put them in a hat, and have the program chair draw the winner or winners of small door prizes at the end of your talk. These prizes can be products you sell, a certificate for service, a free evaluation, etc. Then use the business cards for follow-up and to compile mailing lists.

> FRIPPICISM
>
> *If you speak to fifty people at a service club, you will eventually do business with more people than you would if you met them one-on-one.*

Your object is to stay in people's minds without bugging them. Use high-tech, low-tech, and no-tech contact techniques. Send lots of thank-you notes, congratulations on promotions, interesting clippings with a note "F.Y.I." Offer free articles to trade and association publications. Become involved with charities and civic causes. Be ongoing and consistent in your efforts to increase your visibility and connections.

Six Quick Tips

1. Vary your energy and intensity.

2. Never open by thanking the audience for having you. It wastes your precious initial thirty seconds, and what if they walk during your presentation?

3. Can anyone else say it? Don't use a poem, story, or joke they've heard before. Be original.

4. Add drama to your stories. Edit them to the nub.

5. Don't be the hero of all your stories. An audience member told me she liked me, but "hates most motivational speakers, because all they do is tell everyone how great they are."

6. If your audience has really been great, thank them at the end. (Bill Gove, the first President of the National Speakers Association, says, "A standing ovation says more about the audience than the speaker.")

Bombing in Front of an Audience

Boo Bue, now retired, told me about a truly terrible speaking experience. "I used to do some talks for Remington Rand, about a ten- or fifteen-minute memorized speech that went with a film on office procedure. One day—I'll never forget it—at the University of Hawaii, they had to block off the windows to make it dark. The building wasn't air-conditioned, so it soon got warm and uncomfortable. And then the picture was not synchronized with the sound. It was a mess.

"By this time, I really became nervous. Then I got up to speak, and the chairman—I couldn't believe it—put a piece of paper in my hands and said, 'Would you please cover these three points.'

"Well, it should have been easy but it wasn't my memorized talk. Have you ever been really embarrassed in front of a group? A physical change came over me. In the Dale Carnegie courses I later taught, I could really empathize with people because of that experience. My stomach was churning. I knew my heart was going through my coat. My voice was up about three octaves. It was terrible.

"The next day I was in downtown Honolulu in a coffee shop. In those days, Honolulu was a very small community. You saw everybody you knew downtown. I ran into someone who had been in the audience the day before. I thought I would go up to her and say, 'Well, I didn't do so well,' and I imagined her replying, 'Oh, you were all right.' People always do that."

"So, I walked up to her and said, 'I didn't do so well,' and she said, 'Yes, you were awful.' My heart dropped. She was a nice person, not one you would think would be so blunt. Then she said, 'You ought to attend Dale Carnegie.' That was my turning point. The first year after taking the training, I doubled my income. The course increased my confidence that much."

Needless to say, my friend Boo never found himself in a similarly distressing situation. He went on to become an international management trainer and Dale Carnegie sponsor for Hawaii and San Francisco.

Those of us in business must stay on our toes. Whenever we get the feeling that everything is great, it's time to take a look around. As Max Gunther says in *The Luck Factor*, "Never, never, never assume you are fortune's darling. Lucky people are those who adapt to an environment of uncertainty....I don't believe that in business or in life you can ever just coast."

YOUR ASSIGNMENT:
Promoting Myself

FRIPPICISM

Quote yourself—not just dead white men.

If I were a powerful, eloquent speaker, which three people or organizations would I like to influence?

How could speaking formally before an audience improve my business life?

How could speaking confidently and persuasively in personal situations improve my private life?

CHAPTER 17

When Things Go Wrong

FRIPPICISM
Things are not as bad as they seem, *They are worse. They are also* *better. We do not see life as it is,* *but as we perceive it to be.*
Robert Fripp

"How many of you have had things go wrong in your business that seemed devastating at the time?" I asked an audience of Women Entrepreneurs in San Francisco. Everyone raised a hand. Some put up two hands.

I have had wonderful businesses, great employees, and many successes. I have also been disappointed, had hard-earned funds embezzled, and had people quit at the most inopportune moments. I managed to live through every single experience and grow from them.

It's relatively easy to look back at business disappointments and realize they were just part of a regular up-and-down cycle. When you survive a few such cycles, you become a lot more valuable to your clients. Personal disasters are also part of the inevitable cycle called life. That's why the more we experience, the more philosophical we become about events, both business and personal, that would have been shattering when we were younger.

Larry Wilson, co-author of *The One Minute Salesperson*, believes most business traumas will turn out to be merely inconveniences or even springboards to something better, as soon as we can see them in perspective. I serve my audience better because of my ability to adapt to both the successes and failures I've experienced.

Adversity in business can stimulate creative thinking and new growth. One man, for example, found himself with a warehouse full of canned white salmon. Housewives, used to the pink kind, spurned it until he had new labels printed: "Snowwhite Alaskan Salmon, guaranteed not to turn pink in the can."

Great thinkers and creative people throughout history have thrived in periods when their work had some sort of restriction put on it: political, financial, or cultural. The symphony and the sonnet are very rigid forms, yet we have an abundance of great symphonies and sonnets. Great works have been produced in hard times, in the midst of hunger, calamity, and oppression. Sometimes a disaster can simply be a restriction that channels us and simplifies our choices.

What if the restriction is physical? Pint-sized Agnes DeMille was too short for a career as a dancer, so she became one of this century's most noted choreographers. Actor Christopher Reeve, filmdom's "Superman," switched from acting to directing when he broke his neck in a 1995 riding accident and was paralyzed from the neck down.

The One-Armed Ball Player

My friend Boo Bue told me the story of George Quam. Boo met George at the Minneapolis Athletic Club in 1961. As a boy, George and his two brothers roamed all over their Minnesota farm. A train track crossed one corner of the property, and George's mother constantly warned her children not to go near the tracks. But as most kids do, George did.

When George was about eight years old, he and his brother were on top of a boxcar playing cowboys and Indians. All of a sudden, a switch engineer hit the cars and George fell between two moving boxcars. Before he could scamper off the track, one of the cars severed his left arm. Quam told Boo, "I was handicapped. If there was any doubt in my mind, that doubt was erased every Saturday when I went to town and behind my back heard everyone say, 'There goes the poor Quam boy. Isn't it a shame the way he's handicapped?'

"Well," Quam said, "handicapped was exactly how I felt. That was my attitude. I didn't have any goals or dreams. I had trouble communicating. I became a loner. Then one day my dad said, 'George, you're going to do the same chores around here your brothers are doing.' I started doing things, and one day I realized I could do everything with one hand that my brothers could do with two. My life was never the same."

In high school, George liked sports. He got letters in football, basketball, and baseball, three years in a row. After high school, he moved to Minneapolis and got a room in a downtown YMCA. He went into real estate and insurance work and was very successful.

One day at the YMCA he saw some people playing handball. He had never seen the game before, so he went down to the handball court and began hitting the ball. He was awkward, but he could do it. About fifteen minutes later, the athletic director came by, saw George, and said, "You can't play handball with one arm! It takes two hands, two arms, a lot of coordination. You ought to take up something like chess or bridge where you can use your mind." George was devastated. That night he didn't sleep, he cried. But the next morning he swore to himself that he was going to play handball.

He got the best players in the club to show how to make the kill shots into the corners. In three years he was the Class A singles champion of Minneapolis YMCA. Then he started playing at the Minneapolis Athletic Club where the competition was even keener...and he set an amazing record. He was the Singles Champion in Class A play for twenty-five straight years.

When Boo met George, Boo was thirty-eight years old and George was sixty-three. "We had just finished playing two games of handball," Boo recalls. "I had some advantages over him. I was younger, I had two arms and two hands, and I could play the game—I had three trophies in my den from the Minneapolis Athletic Club. Yet he beat me 21-4, 21-5, and I think he gave me all nine points. In other words, he murdered me. And I said to him, 'George, I figured you'd beat me, but I didn't think you'd beat me this easily.' He said, 'Well, I have a big advantage over you. Every time you went over to the left, you wondered whether you should hit the ball with your left hand or backhand with your right. I never have to take the time to make that decision.'

"To me, it was a remarkable way of doing what Dale Carnegie says, 'When life hands you a lemon, make lemonade.' George made a positive out of a negative. As we left the athletic club that day, I asked him about his philosophy of life. I'll never forget his answer. He said, 'Boo, it's not what you have that counts, but what you do with what you have.'"

The Woman Who Changed the Law

Susan Helmrich and I met on an airplane flying to Toronto. It turned out she had planned to hear me speak two nights before, but she hadn't made it. I make it a policy not to engage in long discussion on airplanes, but Susan and I talked nonstop for five hours until the plane landed. Susan is one of those spunky people who got a raw deal in life. Instead of withdrawing into self-pity, she fought to help others in the same situation.

Susan was twenty-one years old, attending college on an athletic scholarship. "I felt fine, although I had had lots of gynecological problems. The day the doctor told me I had cancer, I was sure he had me mixed up with another patient. It couldn't be me. He said, "Yes." And I said, "Is it serious?" He said, "Yes." And I said, "Will I be able to have children?" He said, "No." That's when I cried. You can't imagine what it's like to lose this option when you're only twenty-one with your whole life ahead of you. Two weeks later I had ten hours of surgery.

Susan learned she was a DES daughter, one of a group of cancer-prone women whose mothers had taken the drug diethylstilbestrol, commonly called DES, in the 1950s. DES was then commonly prescribed to prevent miscarriage during pregnancy, although it was never tested for this use and was found to be totally ineffective in preventing miscarriage. At first Susan concentrated on surviving from day to day.

"When all that is happening to you, you don't think about lawsuits or of suing anyone. All you can think about is getting well. I spent one month in the hospital, and after that I had two subsequent major abdominal surgeries. It was a long, hard road, but somehow I kept on going. I was hospitalized ten times in three years. Every time I started to feel good and think I was cured, I'd end up back in the hospital with complications. But, I had lots of support. My family, my friends, and my doctors and nurses were always there for me and helped me a lot.

"When I decided to go to graduate school, people were incredulous. But you can sit in your room by yourself for the rest of your life, or you can get on with your life."

In 1978, Susan started her master's degree at Harvard in epidemiology. She also tried to file a lawsuit against the manufacturers of DES. She learned that, under New York state law, the statute of limitations had run out. In 1979, she and other DES daughters began lobbying to change the law.

"We started as six women. We quickly realized we weren't strong enough to fight the New York State Senate. We had to gather more support. We used media coverage and joined the Toxic Victims Coalition, which included those exposed to asbestos and other harmful substances."

As Susan's political savvy grew, she also learned how to cope with her own feelings. "An important thing is to allow yourself to cry. Acknowledge it's a horrible thing you're going through. Finally, I was able to say, 'This is horrible; I hate this; I'm depressed.' I had felt I needed to be strong for everybody else, but that's not true. You have to be strong for yourself. I've grown a lot because if I could endure that, I know I can do anything."

Each year Susan's lobbying group was faced with new barriers, but year after year, they slowly gathered support from other organizations. By 1985, they had the support of the AFL-CIO and many victims of toxic exposures.

"My wedding was scheduled for June 15, 1986, but I spent the early part of June 1986 lobbying in Albany. It seemed as though another year would end in defeat. Then I got married and left for my honeymoon in Hawaii with my new husband. Our second day there, we got a phone call that the bill had passed. It seemed like a fantasy because here we were off on this beautiful island. I couldn't believe it.

"A few weeks later I was asked to fly to New York for the bill-signing ceremony with Governor Cuomo and Robert Abrams, Attorney General of New York. Two other victims were asked to be present: an asbestos widow and a man with heavy metal disease. The day of the bill signing was a day I'll never forget. I saw the culmination of six years of hard work. I was talking to the media about having had cancer surgery which meant I'd never be able to have children. I cried when the bill was signed because I was ecstatic, and I was also sad that the whole reason I was there was because I had had cancer and all these terrible things had happened to me. But the new law allows me to seek compensation."

Susan went on to complete her master's degree at Harvard and earn a doctorate in epidemiology from the University of California, Berkeley. "Looking back," she says, "the legislative work I did has been the most rewarding of my life because I was able to help change a law that will affect thousands and thousands of people. And that's a good feeling."

The Ultimate Loss

Judith Briles is the successful author of eighteen books including *Financial Savvy for Women, Raising Money-Wise Kids, Gendertraps*, and *The Dollars and Sense of Divorce*. She is also someone who has fought her way back from two major losses. Several years ago, her business partner embezzled over half a million dollars that Judith had to cover, and she lost her home, cars, and every asset she had.

The second loss was more devastating. Her nineteen-year-old son, Frank, died in a tragic accident. He was climbing on the old Dumbarton Bridge in the San Francisco Bay with some friends, somehow mis-stepped, and toppled over the side. He hit a girder on the way down, and then was swept away by the outgoing tide. His body was recovered seven weeks later.

"Frank was the kind of kid whose gift to me on Mother's Day was cleaning his room," Judith recalls. "Our life felt pretty good. Frank had a bank account, had saved some money, and was going to buy a new motorcycle. It was Labor Day weekend. We had dinner, then he and his friends all went off to the movies. At 1:00 a.m. I got up and saw that my youngest daughter's door was still open. My first thought was to wring her neck because she had no business being out that late. Frank's door was closed and so was my oldest daughter's door, so I assumed they were both in. I went back to bed.

"Two hours later I bolted straight up. My younger daughter was at the foot of the bed and I remember saying, 'What do you mean, Frank is in the morgue?' She led me down the hallway, into the brightly lit family room where a lone policeman stood. He said, 'I'm sorry, there's been an accident.'

"Because I was well known, the story was all over the newspapers. I couldn't retreat into private grief the way I had when I lost a newborn baby years before. And there were ten friends with Frank when he died, including his younger sister. We had a lot of work to do with these young people to help them deal with their first tragedy.

"As time went by, I continued to withdraw. I'd go into work, but I was encased in a shell. It was strange. Everyone assumed I was doing well, but I wasn't doing well at all. It was a long time before anyone realized the crisis that had encircled me.

I was in the middle of my studies for my doctorate, and I was having nightmares about Frank."

Outwardly, Judith seemed fine, so few realized how bad off she had become. She began to experience frequent memory loss. She forgot to bring her checkbook when she went shopping, forgot to carry money for bridge tolls, forgot to pay bills so the phone was cut off.

Her relationship with her husband, John, Frank's stepfather, was deeply strained. She turned her anger on him, imagining all the things he'd failed to do with Frank, and it took a lot of work to rebuild their relationship. Her daughters, who had been ready to go off on their own, recognized her unresolved grief, and decided to stay and support her. "We decided to all hang together," says Judith. "Now we're probably the best we've ever been. What came out of that tragedy could have wiped everything out, but it didn't.

"During that journey, my son left me three gifts: first, a renewed spirituality; second, his joyous sense of being a little kid. I've taken that as part of myself now. I mean I really want to have fun. I like having fun. I've always liked having fun, but now I'm serious about having fun. And third, touching base with and reaffirming my own values.

"I've had a lot of growth since that time, and I have learned from my own personal situation that no matter how much money I might lose, how badly my career may be hurt, it doesn't matter. Family counts most. Nothing else could hurt me. I have my priorities in the correct order now."

Judith's ordeal demonstrates three points about surviving:

1. Any great loss involves loss of part of yourself, so realize it will take time to rebuild.

2. Loss can force you to redefine your priorities and goals, to refocus, and to renew.

3. You can rebuild.

The Road Back

Author/lecturer Joan Minninger was devastated when her husband and business partner died. Although she carried on so that few noticed any change, she was really operating on automatic. After two years, she recognized she was ready to start again. She threw a party and invited all the people who had ever hired her, ostensibly to thank them but privately to celebrate that her grieving was over. The party was a tremendous success on both fronts.

The Phone Call in the Night

Many people have things happen in their lives they can't predict, didn't cause, didn't want, and can't avoid.

Pat Wiklund was a successful, well-known therapist, married to another successful, well-known therapist, and the mother of a precious son. Just before the event that changed her life, she had attended her high school's twentieth reunion. Comparing her life since graduation with those of her classmates, Pat decided she had done pretty well. "Boy, did I feel smug! I knew I had it made! Here I was in a long-term marriage with a child that was the absolute apple of our eye. A house we had just purchased and remodeled. I was just starting to achieve real career success."

But within a few months it was all gone. A ringing phone woke her very early one morning. "I was so sleepy, it took me a few moments to realize the other side of the bed, next to the phone, was empty. I got up to answer it and heard a man's voice at the other end. I had no idea who it was, but he was crying. Then I realized it was my husband. He was telling me he had been arrested and was in jail. Later that day, our attorney told us we were going to have a hundred days of hell. He was wrong. It turned out to be almost a thousand.

"The charge against my husband was sexual molestation of a child. It was all a terrible mistake, of course. My first reaction was to take charge and take care of my husband. He worked with disturbed children, and some of them must have invented this story because of their illness. He kept assuring me he was innocent, and I believed him totally.

"But the charges were true. My husband was both a child psychologist and a preferential child molester. For years, he had targeted a specific type of child and literally seduced and ensnared that child. My whole safe, familiar, fulfilling world collapsed.

"The worst part of what happened to me—and what happens to a lot of people whose worlds are shaken by such challenges—is that others say, "You must have done something to make this happen." Friends and relatives told me, "If only you'd been different, if you hadn't been so demanding, if you hadn't been such a strong woman, he'd never have done that." No one suggested any personal responsibility on his part. It was all my fault. I was stunned. What had I done to deserve this? *Had* I done something?

"Finally it dawned on me that blaming the victim is a natural, if reprehensible, human response. People reason, 'If she didn't know, if she didn't do something to cause this, then maybe there's something terrible going on in my own life that I'm not causing and I'm not aware of, something that's waiting to pounce on me.' It's much safer and more comfortable to blame the victim: 'Aw, she really knew about it all the time. She was in denial and not paying attention. But something like this could *never* happen to me!'"

In her guilt and fear that she might have deserved the blame others were fixing on her, she ultimately recognized a pattern common to sufferers of personal catastrophe. Regardless of religious beliefs, she notes, these people go through a "crisis of faith" in which they ask themselves, "What have I done to bring this kind of pain? How did I create this? How did I enable this?" Pat learned to see past these feelings to the truth of her husband's responsibility for hurting others, not only the children and their families, but herself and her son.

Her husband's criminal charges were only the beginning. Soon there were expensive and exhausting civil suits filed by the victims, ultimately paid by malpractice insurance. Friends now came forward with suspicious incidents they had witnessed that had seemed perfectly innocent at the time. Pat's husband still continued to deny everything, but the proof was indisputable. Finally Pat understood her husband wasn't going to change, and she filed for divorce. Her lawyer recommended that she not mention the molestation charges, saying this was such a common accusation in divorce cases that the judge might assume she was lying and hold it against her!

Pat's recovery and regrowth has been a complex process. Most of all, she depended on the support of her sister. Ultimately, as part of the healing, she chronicled her new knowledge in a book called *Sleeping with a Stranger: How I Survived Marriage to a Child Molester*. Everyone has enormous sympathy for the victims of child abuse and their families; many try to understand the abuser; but few have considered that the family of the abuser are also damaged by the tragedy. When Pat's in-laws heard she was writing a book about her experiences, they threatened to cut their grandchild off from a sizable inheritance if it was published. Pat discussed this with her son, who said, "Mother, go ahead." The story of her healing process has helped many regain their feet after unexpected devastation.

"We make so many assumptions," says Pat. "There are the predictable developmental changes no one likes but everyone gets to do: our kids grow up; our parents die; our bodies age. However, it's the imposed changes that no one likes, the things we can't predict, the ones we don't cause, the things you don't want but can't avoid. Those are the ones that can make us crazy.

"Our choices about our next step depend on how we define what's happening right now. Find out what's really going on. Find experts, people who think differently than you, so you can discover that there's another way the world works. You're not going to like what they have to say, but 'denial isn't just another river in Egypt.' The tough part about being labeled as 'in denial' is that it's very hard to know what you don't know, particularly when you're dealing with a situation you never imagined someone like you would ever have to deal with: your kid may be on drugs; your husband may be cheating on you; your business partner may have cleaned out your coffers and fled to Brazil. But as long as you assume people like you will never have to associate with people like that, you don't have the information you need. It's tough to listen to the yucky stuff over and over. I call this the Nine Sober Russians Rule. If nine sober Russians keep telling you you're drunk, you better lie down until you're sure. You can't always trust how you feel and think when you're in such a situation.

"Someone said to me, 'Pat, when this is all over, you'll appreciate the pain.' Baloney! You never appreciate it. But I'm not the same woman who got that telephone call at eight o'clock that morning. My life is dramatically different. But it's a lot more fun, a lot more satisfying in this version than that."

After the Deluge

We all want to be able to choose, but it doesn't always happen that way. It didn't for Venita VanCaspel. "I was happily married," Venita says, "when one day my husband took a business trip on the Braniff Electra. The wing fell off and everyone was killed. For a while I said 'Why? Why?' We were clean, went to church, and did all those beautiful things, and I kept saying, 'Why, Lord?' But when I finally discovered I wasn't going to get an answer, I quit asking. Next, I went through a period when I said, 'Lord, there must be a reason you left me here alone with so much of my life still ahead of me. You must have a blueprint for me. Just show me what the blueprint is and I'll do it.'

"But that's not the way the Lord works either. He doesn't lay out the whole blueprint for us to see. I began to feel that as I took one step, I would know the next step, like going down a pathway at night with a lantern. You can't see the end of the path, but if you take the next step you can see to take the next step, and the next step. Finally, you arrive where you should be.

"And this was the way it was with me. I kept taking the next step. I had received some life insurance upon the death of my husband. I had a degree in economics and a degree in finance—a lot more education than the average woman had at that time—yet I hadn't been taught what to do with money. So I went back to college and studied investments, learning what to do with my money. All that time, I was searching for something worthwhile to do with my life.

"I decided to be a stockbroker. That seems simple enough, but in 1961 in Houston, Texas, it wasn't. A woman stockbroker? No such thing. I went from firm to firm to firm, and they all said, 'We tried a woman once and it didn't work.' (Of course, men also dropped out daily without being singled out by sex.) I finally got out the rules of the New York Stock Exchange and read them. You would be amazed at what they said. They said you had to work for a member firm six months and pass the test. Period. That's all the rules said. So I got a job in the back office of a brokerage firm, and I sent off for a correspondence course. I studied the Exchange rules. At the end of the six months, I told the firm I worked for that I'd like to take the examination. They called me a crackpot. I said again that I'd like to take the exam. Thinking I couldn't pass it, they finally agreed. I took it and I passed.

"The brokerage firm now had a bigger problem: what to do with me. I remember the boss calling me in. He cleared his throat and he said, 'I think we'll throw you in the water and see if you can swim. I'll tell you what that means. It means we carry the men on a draw [give them a salary] for a year, but we're not going to give you any money. If you need anything, ask for it.' That was my training program. But you can learn to swim if you just have the courage to hop in the water."

Venita VanCaspel became a successful stockbroker before there *were* women stockbrokers and is still at the top of her profession today.

You Still Have Them

One of the realities of life is that our parents are probably going to die before we do. We grow up, and then suddenly they're not there anymore. Both my parents are dead, but my brother and I like to say we still have them. We just don't enjoy their company.

The same is true of all our past experiences. I've been accused of having a Walt Disney philosophy. Yes, things can go wrong. Yes, we can lose things tremendously important to us. Sometimes we can work hard and get them back. Sometimes this is impossible. But we always have them just the same, locked in our memories and reflected in our attitudes and achievements.

FRIPPICISM

Life is what we're given.
Living is what we do with it.

Robert Fripp

If we are wise, our memory will not be a prison, but a storehouse of wealth to draw on for the rest of our lives. My brother wrote, "Probably nothing gives life its keenness and poignancy so much as the presence of death and dying. The death of one's mother hits about as close to home as you can get. But the death of friendship and trust also reminds us of the richness which both bring to life and our living of it. The quality of our dying reflects the quality of our living. The quality of our living determines the quality of our dying. May my living honor my parents. May my living honor my family and friends. May my living repay the debt of my existence."

YOUR ASSIGNMENT:
What Would I Do If My World Fell Apart?

FRIPPICISM

Looking back at what might have been gets in the way of what can be.

If tragedy struck tomorrow, how would I cope?

On whom would I call for help?

For information?

For comfort?

What beliefs and inner strengths would I draw on?

CHAPTER 18

Your Love Affair with Life

> **FRIPPICISM**
>
> *If you don't have a romance with yourself, it will be a lot tougher to have a romance with other people and with life.*

More than anything else, people ask me, "How can I know what I want? I'm intelligent and well educated," they say. "I have a good job and I'm not unattractive. But how can I know what I want?"

My reply is a question. "If in five years you are doing exactly what you're doing now, in the same job, with the same company, with the same friends—if you look the same, and you spend your free time doing the same things—will you be happy?" If the answer is no, then the next question is, "What would make you happy?"

If you don't want to look the way you do now, what goals can you establish for gaining or losing weight, developing better muscle tone, better grooming, a new outlook reflected in the clothes you wear and how you wear them? If you don't like certain character traits, what can you do to change them? You don't have to set monumental goals to make a difference in your life.

If you would not be happy in the same job five years from now, look within your company or organization for other jobs. Are there other departments? Higher positions? Could you create a new department or position? How far can you go? If you like the possibilities in your company, figure out what you have to learn, whom you have to impress, whom you have to know, and what you have to do. If you are not satisfied with the possibilities in your organization, look around your field. Is there anything else out there for you? Think about your talents, your abilities, your interests. What other things could you do? If the options in your field don't appeal to you, start talking to people in other industries.

Take Inventory

If you don't have a strong sense of your talents and interests, have your abilities tested to determine your aptitudes. Are you mechanically minded? Are you analytically inclined? Do you work well with numbers? Are you creative? Do you like to work with other people? Do you like to work alone? These are the things you must know about yourself.

Think about your personal life. Are you happy single or married? How would you like your personal and social life to be different? How can you make your marriage, your family, your living situation better?

The important thing is to think. And as Leo Rosten once said in the *Saturday Review*, "Thinking is harder work than hard work."

Love Affairs

People in love secrete extra hormones that make the whole world seem rosier. Starting a new job often feels almost as exciting. But the real story begins after the conclusion of the fairy tale, "and they lived happily ever after."

Remember how exciting it was the first time you fell in love? Your heart did somersaults every time you met the object of your affection. The two of you sat up talking all night, and you always seemed to have so much energy. The thrill of falling in love was wonderful.

Soon enough, reality set in and you had to start working to make the relationship succeed. That's good, of course. It's how you grow to truly know and love the other person. In many ways, a new job is also a love affair, and it goes through the same three stages.

The first stage, excitement, can last from one hour to many years. You think to yourself: This job will pay me more money than I've ever earned before; the clients will be wonderful to deal with; I'm going to learn so much and do exciting things. The novelty of the job keeps your energy high, and you are very productive because you are happy. In fact, being productive makes you happy.

The second stage is reality, the end of the honeymoon. No more rose-colored glasses. You still enjoy the work, but you begin to notice the things you *don't* like. Perhaps getting up early every morning or coming into an office of madly ringing phones. Suddenly, you're keenly aware of the less-than-perfect aspects that you had overlooked before.

The third stage, for both jobs and love affairs, is noticing the greener grass elsewhere. You start looking for other things to occupy your mind besides how to make more out of the situation or relationship you are in. You notice all the negatives, and that's when the maybes begin. "Maybe I could make better money at Company X and not have to work so hard," you say. "Maybe I'd be happier with more responsibility in Corporation Y. Maybe Company Z would let me come in a little later in the morning." Just as you put the blame in a relationship on someone else, you come to believe your job has somehow failed you.

This time of re-evaluation is a critical juncture in your relationship with your job (or your partner.) If you think your job has failed, ask yourself a few simple questions.

- Are you giving 100 percent?
- Are you causing your own problems, perhaps to find a little excitement?
- Are you worried about the future of your company and the part you play in it?
- Do you feel unappreciated?
- Why did you take that job in the first place?
- What were the things that first attracted you? Are they still a part of your daily experience? Why don't they thrill you anymore?
- What things have disappointed you? How important are they?

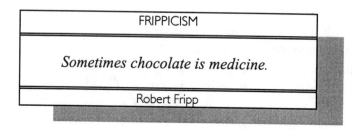

FRIPPICISM

Sometimes chocolate is medicine.

Robert Fripp

Pretend You Own the Company

The most important thing your job can offer you is a chance to feel good about yourself. Do you see yourself as a productive, contributing member of the company? Do you know why your company exists? When you realize what your company offers to society, you'll be able to understand what part you play.

Work with the attitude that you own the company that employs you. You earn your money from your employer by doing more than you are paid to do. According to the law of sow and reap, you will get noticed for being an exceptional worker, so never worry about giving your employers something for nothing. More important, you'll feel good about yourself because you will be a productive person with a part in your company's future. Reaping the rewards of self-satisfaction, no matter what you are paid, is the true measure of the work you do, whether in love, your career, or your life.

The best maxim for achieving success in your job, your relationships, and every other aspect of your life is the universal parable about sowing and reaping. The successes you reap in life are the results of the positive energy and hard work which you have sown in the past—a past that you can begin building immediately in the present, for rewards in the future.

Love in a Less-Than-Perfect World

Reality rarely lives up to expectations. I ask my clients, "What message do you want me to get across that you would tell your people if you could?" They invariably answer, "Tell them it's the same everywhere else. Everyone is having to do more with less. Expectations are up in every industry and company."

No company is perfect. As long as you're accepting a paycheck, you should keep your gripes to yourself and concentrate on some of the positive things about your company.

Bobbie Gee, corporate image consultant, traveled home to southern California from Chicago on a flight plagued with problems from beginning to end. The plane was three hours behind schedule. One of the cargo doors was frozen, and there was no food in first class. The man sitting next to her complained all the way about how this airline could do absolutely nothing right. Who was he? A pilot for the same airline!

What was wrong with this picture? First, the pilot diminished his own company by running it down. Second, the company had a bigger problem than delays and cargo door malfunctions: it has at least one antagonistic worker whose criticisms had no outlet but the ear of the public. What do you think are the chances the company and its pilot will prosper? Will the company grow? Will the employee be happy with his job and his life? Moral: *All love affairs need two-way communication.*

Rekindling the Spark

It's very important to be centered in reality, in love or in a job. In any relationship, you have to work to feel the excitement on a continuing basis. You need excitement in your life. What did you do to keep the thrill in your love relationship? Perhaps the two of you relived your first date at that little country restaurant. Perhaps you thanked your loved one for just being there for you. Whatever you did, you got in touch with the person you first fell in love with.

The same kind of techniques, applied to your career, can rekindle the excitement you felt when you began your job. You must have had good reasons for taking the job in the first place. What were they? Make a list of them and start experiencing those things again in your daily routine.

In Japan, workers gather each morning to cheer their company before they go to their work stations. It's hard to imagine rows of corporate American employees doing the same thing, but you can lead your own personal cheering section. Begin each day expecting to have a productive, exciting day. Wasn't that how you used to arrive at your job in the morning? If you really expect to be productive during the day, very little will keep you from it.

There are many ways we can keep both personal relationships and jobs exciting and challenging, while still being realistic. Ultimately, of course, your happiness depends on how you feel about yourself in the context of your job, a relationship, or just plain living. It's too easy to get trapped by immediate goals. Stay aware of what is out there on the horizon. When plans don't seem to be working, adjust your actions and expectations.

There are rewards for virtue just as there are costly punishments for shirking our duties. I see virtue in the effort of each of us to find ourselves, to make ourselves useful, to set our goals, to go about our work and our lives. Duty doesn't mean a loss of freedom, because duty requires self-discipline, and self-discipline is the key to personal freedom.

Balancing on the High Wire

Have I had it all? No, but I've had everything I wanted. The reality of my own life today far exceeds my wildest expectations. You ask, "So you have a great life, but what's the message for me?" Here's my message: Turn your disadvantages into advantages. Always turn up. Develop excellent work habits. And accept temporary imbalance while striving for balance over the long haul.

The Mystical Click

Making ourselves available to opportunities represents a major breakthrough in our adult life. A child will look at the funny symbols under the pictures in books and suddenly realize they have meaning. Similarly, we can hear over and over about how we control our own lives, and yet we never really believe it until suddenly something clicks. All the axioms, clichés, and vaguely perceived ideas suddenly shift and come into sharp focus, creating a vivid, three-dimensional picture of who we are and where we are going. When we make ourselves available to opportunity, we put ourselves that much closer to this realization. It is this "click," this near-mystical moment, that changes us forever. I hope this book is the click you need. Remember what Fripp stands for:

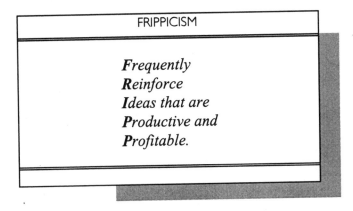

FRIPPICISM

Frequently
Reinforce
Ideas that are
Productive and
Profitable.

Put the best ideas to work...starting now.

INDEX

BEST SELLERS FROM EXECUTIVE BOOKS
1-800-233-BOOK

7 Secrets of Exceptional Leadership by Christopher J. Hegarty & Philip B. Nelson   **$13.99**
To be a leader today one must abandon many traditional concepts of leadership and excel at understanding specific new skills necessary to succeed.

The Road To Happiness—Is Full Of Potholes by Tim Connor   **$11.95**
So, you want to be happy!! So do 4 billion people in the world. Join the happy club! The Road to Happiness is about: Where you can find happiness, Where you can't find happiness; Who is responsible for your happiness; Who isn't responsible for your happiness; What happiness is; and What happiness isn't.

Four Star Leadership For Leaders Edited by Charles "T" Jones, CPAE   **$12.95**
28 interviews with 28 Four-Star Generals and Admirals on their style of leadership. General Patton's and The Soldier's Testament quotes are worth the price of the book.

The Great Wing Dr. Louis Tartaglia, M.D.   **$10.00**
"One of the greatest parables I've ever read." Og Mandino
The attitudes for success told through a story of twelve flocks of geese. The *Great Wing* is a living classic that will inspire a pre-teen to prepare for a Tremendous transformational journey. It will encourage those in flight to keep on keeping on using the principles that never fail and those who have arrived will start a new flight of significance teaching the true values that become more beautiful as they are shared.

*Honesty	*Hope	*Faith	*Courage
*Trust	*Spirituality	*Humility	*Willingness
*Perseverance	*Restitution	*Forgiveness	*Service

Five Important Things by Jim Paluch   **$14.95**
Our 1996 best seller and may be our best seller in 1997. "Five Important Things" is an inspirational classic. In an age when everything seems to be changing, here is a tremendous living story reminding us that things that matter never change. The simple concepts that can truly change your life are....

1. Continue to Learn   3. Attitude   5. Don't Quit
2. Appreciate People   4. Set Goals

Stairway To Success Nido R. Qubein, CPAE   **$12.95**
Possibly the best new blueprint for success for everyone. Nido Qubein is not only one of the greatest public speakers, but a practicing businessman with the ability to communicate great truths in the simplest form.

Visions by Ty Boyd, CPAE   **$10.00**
From the Leaders of Today For the Leaders of Tomorrow
Ty Boyd, one of America's great speakers and television personalities, shares the wisdom of leaders he has worked with. Over 100,00 in print.

The Sale-25 High Performance Selling Skills Don Hutson, CPAE   **$15.00**
Don Hutson, one of America's top sales trainers, has put together 500 pages of sales ideas and wisdom."This is a sales classic for every library," quotes Og Mandino.

I'm No Hero by Charlie Plumb, CPAE   **$12.00**
Charles Plumb's story on eight years as a Vietnam P.O.W. has been heard by millions. His book is even better. Some companies have given it to every employee. A tremendous living story of how we depend on each other.

There IS No Joy In Gruntsville Jeff & Ron Hotstetler   **$10.00**
(But there's plenty to learn there)
The real road to the Superbowl. A tremendous story by Jeff and Ron Hostetler of their life-long journey learning to pay the price and the rewards. You don't have to be a sports enthusiast to enjoy and learn from this book. It is a must for every student of leadership. Here are two football role models that write for all of us.

Life Is Tremendous-7 Laws of Leadership by Charles "T" Jones, CPAE   **$ 9.99**
"Life Is Tremendous is a classic ... its powerful message, seasoned with tears and laughter, will continue to change lives for the better, long after this troubled century is only a memory." Og Mandino
Almost 2,000,000 copies in print - English, French, Polish, Spanish

Insights Into Excellence by The Speakers Roundtable $12.00

The quest for Excellence is more than a buzzword today; it is a way of life. Doing something about Excellence is the purpose of this book. Each of the 22 professional speakers presented in this collection is a member of the prestigious Speakers Roundtable. They present timely, practical techniques and philosophies which have worked for other persons and will work for you.

1.	The Role of a Manager	Ken Blanchard
2.	Quick, Before It's Gone: Grabbing Hold of Tommorrow	Ty Boyd
3.	Technology Has Dealt Us a New Deck of Cards	Daniel Burrus
4.	Interviewing: Find "The Natural" in People	Jim Cathcart
5.	Passport to Potential	Danny Cox
6.	Take Charge of Your Future	Patricia Fripp
7.	You Do It To You	Bill Gove
8.	Takin' Up The Slack	Tom Haggai
9.	Stop Hoping and Start Coping	Ira Hayes
10.	The Consistently Exceptional Leader	Christopher Hegarty
11.	The Challenge of Excellence	Art Holst
12.	Management Techniques that Work or Leadership in Action!	Allan J. Hurst
13.	Productivity through Motivation	Don Hutson
14.	Excellence through Humor or Laughter, Thinking and Books	Charlie Jones
15.	Five Keys to Excellence	Jim Newman
16.	Packing Parachutes	Charles Plumb
17.	Position Yourself for Success	Nido Qubein
18.	A Ticket to Anywhere	Cavett Robert
19.	Success is a Journey	Brian Tracy
20.	A Psychologist's Perspective on Excellence	Herb True
21.	The Winning Edge of Excellence	Jim Tunney
22.	Leadership --The Unforged Path	Tom Winninger

You and Your Network by Fred Smith $4.95

Fred Smith is one of this country's greatest thinkers. He waited thirty years to write this book. This would be my pick of all the books for a success guide (Charles "T Jones).

1. You - the person you mean to be
2. Your Heroes - someone to look up to
3. Your Models - choose them carefully
4. Your Mentors - they'll keep you growing
5. Your Peers - winning the Peer-pressure game
6. Your Enemies - they really can be a blessing
7. Your Friends - vital buttresses for our lives
8. Your Family - the ultimate measuring of relationships

Speaking Secrets Of The Masters The Speakers Roundtable $15.00

It is the perfect, comprehensive resource for anyone who needs to share their dreams, ideas and concepts with confidence.

1.	How To Increase Your True Speaking Power	Cavett Robert
2.	A One Minute Course In Public Speaking	Ken Blanchard
3.	Speaking Soul To Soul	Charlie Plumb
4.	How To Get From Fear To Fun	Jim Newman
5.	The Power Of Humor	Herb True
6.	Timing Is Everything	Don Hutson
7.	Speak From your Strengths	Daniel Burrus
8.	What I Teach Some Of America's Most Successful Executives	Ty Boyd
9.	Preparing For Your Speech	Tony Alessandra
10.	Customize Your Style and Content To Fit Your Audience	Jim Cathcart
11.	Setting The Stage For Success: A Before-You-Speak Checklist	Nido Qubein
12.	Creative Storytelling	Naomi Rhode
13.	Tools For The Master Speaker	Charlie Jones
14.	The 12 Biggest Pitfalls To Avoid On The Road To Successful Speaking	Tom Winninger
15.	The Architecture Of Empathy And Effectiveness	Jim Tunney
16.	You've Got To Be Lively Or You'll Lose Them	Patricia Fripp
17.	A Speech Is A Journey	Art Holst
18.	Perils Of The Platform	Danny Cox
19.	So You've Been Asked To Give A Talk	Allan Hurst
20.	Discover The Speaking Power That's Inside Of You	Bill Gove
21.	If You Care, If You Prepare, You Too Can Be A Speaking Success	Brian Tracy
22.	Speaking Is Simple: Just Tell People What You Know	Ira Hayes

The Secret Of Success by R.C. Allen   **$8.00**
Full of wisdom and common sense. This fact-filled book shows you how to increase your desire, get more ideas, eliminate problems, earn more money and bring harmony and joy into your life in many ways.

1. Let There Be Light
2. The Secret Revealed
3. The Wonderful Power You Possess
4. Thy Will Be Done
5. There is No Limit to Your Potential
6. How to Tune in the Infinite Mind
7. The Law of Evolution
8. The Laws of Compensation
9. The Law of Prosperity
10. The Law of Non-Resistance
11. The Wonderful Gift of Choice
12. The Magical Power of Prayer

You Can Do It! by Bob Budler, Foreword by Pat Williams   **$10.95**
Motivational messages from 137 successful men and women in business, education, sports, religion, entertainment, government, industry, and communications.

Quotes Are Tremendous by Charlie "Tremendous" Jones, CPAE   **$10.00**
There is nothing that can empower you more than a Tremendous quote if you want to get their attention quickly and be remembered. Begin with a Tremendous quote, end with a Tremendous quote and season your remarks with Tremendous quotes.

Motivational Classics Foreword by Charles "T" Jones   **$10.00**
This small volume contains three books...three reknown classics that could change your life dramatically.

As A Man Thinketh   *Acres of Diamonds*   *Kingship of Self Control*

The Books You Read Charles "T" Jones
A one minute reader that will help you see the Tremendous power of a book. Each page contains 200 words about a life-changing book.

Og Mandino writes in the Foreword:

"This marvelous book that you are now holding is unique ... a shoppping list, really, to guide you to the very best work that man and woman has written dealing with many areas of your life. Search these pages carefully and I am certain that you will discover exactly the book or books that will help you to deal with your specific problem, whatever it may be. Just think of the time alone that this precious reference will save you in your personal search for the answers you need in order to reach your full potential.

We all need help. There is no such thing as a self-made man or woman. Charles "Tremendous" Jones has performed a miracle through this book. He has created a vehicle, a channel if you will, that will lead you to the perfect specialist that can cure whatever is preventing you from making the progress you deserve. You are a miracle, God's greatest miracle, and now you have a guide that will lead you to the answers you need and prove to yourself, as well as others, how great you really are. Happy hunting, good reading, and joyful living!"

Business Edition   **$14.95**
Leaders from all walks of life, predominately business leaders.

Professional Edition   **$14.95**
Actors, Authors and Althletes, Coaches and Public Speakers

Devotional Edition   **$14.95**
Pastors, Educators, Missionaries, Authors, Evangelists and many of those who shaped the life of the editor, Charles "T" Jones.

Historical Edition   **$14.95**
Presidents, Chief Justices, College Presidents, Military Leaders, Inventors and hundreds of historical figures who made our history.

ORDER FORM

YES! I want _____ copies of "Get What You Want" by Pat Fripp; published by Executive Books at $15.00

Please add $5.00 shipping and handling for the order. Residents of PA also add appropriate sales tax.

ISBN 0-937539-26-0

Call 1-800-233-2665 to order by phone; or by FAX, 1-717-766-6565. Prepayment is required.

_____ Check enclosed

_____ Charge my account:

Visa	Account # _____	Exp Date: ____
MasterCard	Account# _____	Exp Date: ____
AmExp	Account# _____	Exp Date: ____

Signature: _____ (Required for all charges)

Make checks payable to **Executive Books**, 206 W. Allen St., Mechanicsburg, PA 17055

Name: _____

Address: _____

_____

Company: _____

☐ Check box for additional information on quantity discounts available on more than 500 inspirational and motivational books and cassettes